Threat of modern warfare to man and his environment

An Annotated Bibliography

Prepared under the auspices of the International Peace Research Association (IPRA)

unesco

ISBN 92-3-101608-3
French edition 92-3-201608-7
Spanish edition 92-3-301608-0

Published in 1979 by the
United Nations Educational,
Scientific and Cultural Organization
7, place de Fontenoy, 75700 Paris, France

Printed in the Workshops of Unesco

Contents

Contents

Preface

The manufacture and utilization of weapons and problems of disarmament have been central issues for peace research since the emergence of this field among the social sciences. Unesco has supported peace research from the beginning and has continually sought ways to contribute, within its fields of competence, to achieving the objectives established by the United Nations concerning disarmament.

At its seventeenth session, the General Conference of Unesco recommended to the Director-General to encourage research "on the dangers to man and his environment inherent in modern armaments and techniques of warfare" (17 C/Resolution 10.1, Part VI, paragraph 27 (iv)). Through its publications and assistance to peace research projects and institutions, Unesco has tried to encourage research on this subject, which is closely related to the study of the social and economic consequences of the arms race and of disarmament.

One of the obstacles to conducting valid scientific research on a subject like disarmament in many parts of the world, particularly in developing countries, is the profusion of references to published material in developed countries, much of which is difficult to acquire, and the lack of information on the exact content and quality of this material. In order to assist researchers, students and officials in such countries, Unesco has prepared two bibliographies containing reports on the trends in research on the fields covered as well as annotations to the references.

The first of these annotated bibliographies dealt with the Social and Economic Consequences of the Arms Race and of Disarmament and was published in English, French and Spanish as No. 39 in the series "Reports and Papers in the Social Sciences".

The present issue of "Reports and Papers in the Social Sciences" contains a companion bibliography on the subject referred to in the resolution quoted above, namely the dangers to Man and his environment inherent in modern armaments and techniques of warfare. It contains an introduction and a descriptive, annotated bibliography of 117 items. The purpose of this bibliography is to provide an overview of the available sources in order to encourage further research based on the experience and knowledge of the past and the realities and trends of the present. The introduction defines the concept of human ecology with particular reference to military activities, providing thereby a framework for the presentation of the bibliography itself. As the introduction and bibliography show, the subject has been rarely written about and the little that exists is, for the most part, quite recent. It is the hope of Unesco that the present publication will encourage more research, particularly in parts of the world where the environmental perspective of armaments issues has received little attention while the ecological damage of the manufacture and use of weapons has been tremendous.

The understanding of ecosystems and the impact of human conduct on them is essential for human survival and an important task of education and science. Unesco is therefore particularly concerned with the irrational squandering of the scarce resources, both human and material, of the planet while the needs of human beings in the fields of education, science, culture and information continue to increase.

Unesco expresses its warmest thanks to the two authors of this bibliography, who are both connected with the Stockholm International Peace Research Institute (SIPRI). Arthur H. Westing, a forest ecologist, is on leave from Hampshire college in Amherst, Massachusetts, U.S.A. Malvern Lumsden, a social psychologist, carried out part of the work at the International Peace Research Institute, Oslo (PRIO). The entire work was prepared under the auspices of the International Peace Research Association (IPRA), which is responsible for its content. The selection of items for inclusion in the bibliography and the opinions expressed do not necessarily represent the views of Unesco. Designations used do not imply the expression of any opinion whatsoever concerning the legal status of any country or territory, or of the authorities of any country or territory.

Unesco contributes, through bibliographies, reference publications and through research activities on direct assistance to institutions in developing countries, to the development of peace research and to the co-ordination of information and documentation in this area. Information and queries from persons or institutions interested in contributing to this programme are always welcome.

June 1978

Threat of Modern Warfare to Man and his Environment

An Annotated Bibliography

Arthur H. Westing and Malvern Lumsden
Stockholm International Peace Research Institute

INTRODUCTION

The well-being of the human race depends upon the care with which it treats its environment. This environment - shared with all other living things - is beginning to suffer the strains of pollution and other destructive human activities. Moreover, science and technology have advanced to a stage at which Man can threaten the very survival of his species. Indeed, the most spectacular means of such self-destruction are the nuclear and other weapons of mass destruction to be found in the major arsenals of the world. There are numerous additional weapons and military activities capable of doing substantial harm to the environment in both war and peace. Below are outlined some of the basic concepts dealing with Man and nature that will provide a conceptual framework within which to consider the military contribution to the debilitation of the human environment.

Ecology: some basic concepts

Ecology is the study of the interrelationships of living organisms and, especially, of groups of living organisms among themselves and between them and the non-living (or physical) environment. These interrelationships are unified within the framework of an ecological system - or ecosystem - that is comprised of the entire community of interacting living things together with the non-living environment with which they come in contact. Such an ecosystem is considered to be a self-sustaining life-support system that is self-sufficient with the exception of a continuing need for an external source of energy, usually the sun. The living community of the ecosystem, that is, its entire biotic component, is comprised of many populations, each of which is an interacting group of individuals of a separate species of plant or animal. Each of these populations is considered to play some role in maintaining the ecosystem.

Ecology includes the study of the adaptability of populations of plant or animal species - including Man - to a given environment or ecological niche. This process of adaptation occurs on a number of levels. The individuals that comprise the population exhibit physiological or behavioural adaptations to their living environment, that is, to the other individuals in their population and to those of the rest of the community. The population itself adapts over time by means of changes in its gene pool, brought about largely through natural selection. Most plant and animal populations show remarkable degrees of physiological, anatomical and morphological specialization, for the most part the result of genetic adaptation over many generations to a particular ecological niche. For human populations, on the other hand, the behavioural adaptations, both individual and organizational, are of greater importance.

A number of complex and in some instances fragile processes must be maintained in perpetuity in order for an ecosystem to maintain its continuing life-support function. For example, a continuous cyclical interchange of nutrients must be maintained within and between the living and non-living components of the ecosystem; that is, between the biota on the one hand and the soil, water and air on the other. Nutrient losses by the system must thus be replenished by external inputs to maintain the long-term viability of the system. There must also be a continuing conversion of light energy to chemical energy by the green plants of the ecosystem, in turn followed by repeated transfers of this energy along the intricate food chains within the system. One can readily recognize that anthropogenic and other disturbances might lead to the deterioration and even disintegration of such a system.

These concepts form an appropriate basis for the study of the ecological impact of war and other military activities.

Ecology and military activities

The relationship between military activities and ecology has virtually endless ramifications. Military activities can disrupt ecosystems both in peace and war, both on the battlefield and off it. Such disruption has often in the past been the incidental by-product of a military activity, but is increasingly often also the result of specific intent. Moreover, it can stem from a diversity of energy or material inputs, the results of which can take numerous forms. These include the destruction of existing living or non-living components of the ecosystem or else the introduction of new ones. The impact of the military disruptions can range from local, transitory and mild to widespread, long-lasting and severe.

Disruptive military activities include, inter alia, the employment of such armaments and techniques as nuclear weapons, conventional high-explosive fragmentation bombs, incendiary weapons, chemical agents, biological agents, mechanical means of land-clearing, rain-making agents and other geophysical modifications. They include as well all of the routine environmental insults normally associated with the civil sector of society, among them pollution

of streams and of the lower atmosphere by manu-
facturing processes and of the upper atmosphere
by jet aircraft.

Modern armaments and techniques of warfare
can dissipate their destructive energy or introduce
their destructive agents on the land or in the sea,
in the air or in the space above it. The ecosystems
at risk may be either terrestrial or oceanic and
either arctic, temperate or tropical. The terrestrial ones may be continental or insular, either
forest, grassland or desert; the oceanic ones may
be estuarine, littoral (near-shore), over the continental shelves or within the ocean basins. Damage
may be inflicted either directly or indirectly and
range from subtle to dramatic.

As suggested above, the concept of the ecosystem is a powerful unifying principle of ecology,
but basically it is only a theoretical construct.
This becomes evident when the attempt is made
specifically to relate the concept of the ecosystem
to most actual situations. Indeed, the concept is
fully applicable in nature only to the entire earth,
which can be considered as one huge interacting
life-support system. But for many purposes this
immense global ecosystem is far too cumbersome a
unit with which to deal. Any method of subdivid-
ing the global ecosystem introduces violations of
greater or lesser magnitude of the concept. The
shortcomings notwithstanding, it is highly useful
to divide the global ecosystem into a number of
major climatically determined habitats (sometimes
referred to as life zones or as biomes). In addition to a number of quite specialized categories,
these life zones conveniently include temperate
forest, tropical forest, temperate grassland,
tropical grassland (savanna), desert, tundra,
estuary, shallow ocean and deep ocean. These
entities can be considered as operational ecosystems either in toto or in subunits determined
by the quirks of geography and topography. A
number of further ecosystems, based on human
manipulations, can also be recognized, including
those resulting from various agricultural, horticultural and silvicultural activities as well as urban
and suburban areas.

Many of the operational ecosystems enumerated
above are subject to direct or indirect military
disruption, which can lead to greater tragedy for
some and less for others. The overall degree of
potential calamity for any one of the ecosystems
depends upon a number of factors. To begin
with, different ecosystems are variously vulnerable
to upset. Insular or arid ecosystems, for example,
can be exceedingly species-poor and are thus
intrinsically fragile. Moreover, especially in the
case of islands, some of the species themselves are
ill-equipped to cope with adversity. Some ecosystems, including arctic and alpine ones, are
very slow to recover from disruption owing to the
harshness of the climate or terrain, or to other
factors such as soil fragility. The vulnerability of
other ecosystems hinges upon their overall limited
global extent or to their degree of geographical
fragmentation. Many individual species of plants
and animals require relatively large contiguous
areas of habitat for survival. The ecosystems
associated with them are thereby vulnerable to the
extent that important biotic components are unable
to survive such fragmentation. In fact, some
ecosystems are of particular concern since they
constitute the habitat for species in special need of
protection because of a danger of extinction or for
some other reason. Finally, numerous ecosystems -
either natural or managed to varying degrees - are
of importance inasmuch as human populations
derive food, shelter, clothing and other amenities
from them.

Human ecology

Human ecology is, inter alia, the study of the
ways in which human populations adapt to their
environment. Human beings, in contrast to other
animals or to plants, are endowed with few structural or physiological characteristics that appear to
be adapted to any particular environment. Rather,
Man owes his adaptability largely to his use of
tools and to his forms of advanced social organization made possible by speech and other means of
communication.

Human groups adapt to a particular physical
environment by: (a) using tools to manipulate the
environment; (b) using other physical artefacts
(e.g. dwellings, clothing, ceremonial objects)
which are among the products of such manipulations; and (c) developing social organizations that
co-ordinate the activities of individuals. The
totality of the physical and social attributes of
human groups is known as "culture"; and thus,
for human populations, the ability of the culture to
adapt to changes in the environment is of the
greatest importance. Whereas one culture may be
well adapted to a particular environment, either
the physical attributes or the form of social organization may be little suited to the demands of some
radically different environment thrust upon it. A
second culture may be more able to cope with
changed environmental conditions.

The basic concepts of ecology are readily
applicable to human populations. Human beings,
like other biological organisms, are dependent upon
a continual interchange of nutrients and waste
materials with their ecosystem. Moreover, the
mental development and stability of the human
being are dependent upon the stimulation of the
nervous system by external inputs, especially
those resulting from the individual's own manipulation of his environment. Human societies, like
individuals, are also dependent upon a continual
interchange with the environment. Imbalances in
the interchanges among members of the human
population, or between the group and its environment, may set in motion the decay or disintegration of that society.

Human ecology, therefore, is much more than a
biological science, though biological considerations
form its basis. Human ecology includes the study
of the ways in which Man actually arranges and
constructs his living space by means of greater or
lesser manipulations of nature, ranging from simple
agricultural to automated factory and transportation
systems. Further, human ecology must take
account of social organization as well as of material
and non-material aspects of human culture as
essential intervening variables in the relationship
between Man and nature.

Human ecology and military activities

To study the impact of war and other military
activities on human ecology involves not only the
study of the extent of the physical destruction of

the human environment - whether rural or urban, natural or man-made - but also the effects of this destruction on the human populations involved. If it were not for culture and social organization one would expect more or less of a one-to-one relationship between the amount of physical destruction on the one hand and the decrease in population size as a result of direct casualties, indirect losses through starvation and disease, declining birth rates and so forth on the other. Some human societies have deteriorated under the impact of war, especially where pre-existing structural strains within the social system have been exacerbated. Others have demonstrated a remarkable ability to adapt to extremes of military destruction.

In principle, therefore, the study of the human ecology of war involves a wide range of biological and human sciences. An interdisciplinary study on such a scale is faced with the problem of integration and may lack coherence. Thus a "systems" approach provides a suitable general framework for encompassing the scope of human ecology in its relation to war and other military activities. The following assumptions are among those inherent in such an approach:

1. Human populations are organized into social systems that are more or less well adapted to a certain physical environment. Man's physical environment is partly determined by natural conditions and is partly built and determined by Man himself.

2. A social system interacts with the environment in order to extract food and materials for continued sustenance through the construction of tools and, through them, dwellings and other artefacts. The process of extraction, manipulation and distribution of food and materials (and the consequent division of labour) are regulated by means of social organization.

3. In order for a society to grow and develop it is necessary for the supply of raw materials to exceed current consumption. A surplus may be obtained by reducing current consumption, by reducing wastage, by increasing efficiency of production or by greater extraction. Once a surplus is attained it can be invested in improvements to the social system, in military activities or in other forms of consumption.

4. Outside stress on a social system induces structural strains that can result either in the deterioration of that system or in the strengthening of that system. The direction of the response depends not only upon the nature and magnitude of the external stress, but also upon a number of internal factors such as the size and complexity of the system as well as its flexibility and robustness.

5. Under wartime conditions the social system is called upon to face a variety of substantial problems, including: (a) a reduction in productive manpower; (b) an increase in number of dependants per supporter; (c) a destruction of tools and other artefacts necessary for production; (d) a debilitation or destruction of raw materials and other natural resources; and (e) a destruction of cultural artefacts, such as dwellings or communication systems.

6. In order to cope with wartime problems, a social system can adapt in a number of ways, among them by: (a) accepting lower standards of living; (b) drawing on surplus stocks for current consumption; (c) increasing productivity; (d) distributing resources more efficiently (e.g. by rationing); (e) adopting a more efficient division of labour (e.g. by employing more women or old people in factories); and (f) overcoming or capitulating to the enemy.

Ecological impact of modern armaments and techniques of warfare

In considering the dangers to Man and his environment inherent in modern armaments and techniques of warfare it becomes useful to distinguish among: (a) incidental or indirect environmental effects of warfare; (b) direct or intentional environmental effects of warfare; and (c) environmental effects of non-hostile military activities. Each of these categories is examined in brief.

Incidental or indirect environmental effects of warfare

The use of force is accepted in international law in the case of legitimate self-defence, in so far as it is directed at the military forces of the enemy. However, when such attack is carried out with modern weapons and techniques it is likely to indiscriminately affect the civil population and to cause widespread, long-lasting and severe damage to the environment. Thus, in spite of the continuing efforts in international law and national regulations to circumscribe the effects of such attacks, it is clear that they will frequently result in substantial incidental environmental debilitation.

Nuclear and other weapons of mass destruction have been the object of most of the attention and research on actual or possible environmental effects of warfare. This focus has tended to obscure the need for further study of the destructiveness of such conventional weapons as high-explosive bombs. These can now be directed systematically in massive quantities at large areas, rather than at specific military targets. Indeed, there has been an exponential increase during this century in both the length and depth of battlefields and the conventional firepower available to combat troops. It is probably not generally appreciated that this increase in firepower continues to the present. Front-line troops of the major powers today have about 25 times the firepower of their predecessors in World War II. Some indications of the environmental impact of the massive employment of conventional firepower are provided by the Second Indochina War.

Coupled with the increasing trend towards greater area coverage by conventional weapons is the increasing exploitation of the time dimension by means of delayed-action weapons. These include a multiplicity of land mines as well as conventional munitions fitted with delayed-action fuses. One modern trend is towards the use of "scatterable" mines that can be disseminated in large numbers by aircraft, artillery or rockets. Huge quantities can be delivered either on the battlefield (in order to impede an advancing enemy) or in rear areas (in order to harass the enemy, a tactic that presents a grave danger to the civil population and to the environment). Environmental dangers of delayed-action munitions have been compounded by the unreliability of the fuses used, with the result that they can remain a hazard for a long time into the future. Only recently has any systematic effort been made to begin to study the environmental problem of unexploded munitions.

Direct or intentional environmental effects of warfare

Some techniques of warefare seek to weaken the military forces of an enemy by intentionally destroying or denying their means of existence, usually including those of the civil population, which is thereby prevented from supporting the military forces. Included amongst these techniques of warfare are: blockade; the destruction of crops or water supplies; the destruction of forest sanctuary or cover; the driving of pastoral communities into inhospitable terrain lacking grazing land for their livestock; other forced relocation of populations; the destruction of housing, communication and health facilities; and - most recently - actions that result in the deterioration of the weather. In so far as the environment of the enemy nation rather than its military forces is the direct object of attack, such techniques are appropriately referred to as "environmental warfare".

Environmental effects of non-hostile military activities

A variety of military activities exists that are not in themselves intentionally directed either at an enemy force or at the environment, but which nevertheless cause injury to the environment. Impacts of this kind include: environmental pollution resulting from the production of munitions (both conventional and nuclear) and other military equipment; land use and the consumption of raw materials for military purposes; and damage to the environment resulting from the testing of conventional and nuclear weapons, from the training of troops and from accidents involving military forces.

Contents of the bibliography

The bibliography consists of 117 publications, listed alphabetically by author and all in some fashion pertaining to the relationship between warfare and the human environment. The intent has been to present a representative selection of relevant publications from the world literature. The cited items have originated in 13 nations and, although five languages are represented, all but seven of the cited items are in English. Most are of quite recent origin, with 73 having been published during the 1970s and another 27 during the 1960s. No comparable bibliography has been published, although a number of tangential ones should be noted, those by: O'Callaghan, 1973; Popper & Lybrand, 1960; Schultz, 1966; and Westing, 1974; q.v.

Of the military activities covered in the bibliography, descriptions or speculations on the use of nuclear weapons have been the most frequent, with those on conventional high-explosive bombs second. Of the habitats examined, tropical forest and the urban environment (especially European cities) have been the most common. Of the wars referred to, the Second Indochina War has been the most usual, followed by World War II. It has, of course, not been possible to provide references to the effects of all kinds of military activity on all kinds of ecosystems, for lack of cases or published information on them. For example, much more research has been devoted to military effects on the environments of major industrial powers than to effects on those of other societies. The frequency distribution of subject-matter in the bibliography is thus in part a reflection of the inequitable distribution of research facilities and funds.

Bibliography

1. AARTSEN, J.P.v.: Consequences of the war on agriculture in the Netherlands. International Review of Agriculture 37, 1946: 5S-34S, 49S-70S, 108S-123S.

Some 10 per cent of the productive land area of the Netherlands sustained severe military damage during World War II, including saltwater inundation, freshwater inundation, mine laying, and pre-emption for fortifications and airfields. The author provides a detailed analysis of these and other direct and indirect war damages to Dutch agriculture, horticulture and silviculture and discusses the problems of reconstruction. One of the most important studies of its kind.

2. Air University Quarterly Review: Attack on the irrigation dams in North Korea. Air University Quarterly Review /now Air University Review/ 6 (4), 1953-1954: pp. 40-61.

A description of and justification for the United States air attacks in 1953 on the irrigation dams of North Korea during the Korean War. This article includes photographs and maps indicating the extent of damage caused by breaching the Toksan, Chasan and other dams. In addition to the tactical gain of destroying communications in the river valleys, the raids were intended to destroy thousands of hectares of growing rice as well as farms and irrigation canals, thereby turning North Korea from an exporter of rice to an importer at a time when intelligence reports indicated a serious rice famine in South China, a possible source of supplies. In addition to "inestimable" damage to the rice crops, the floods caused extensive damage to the capital city, Pyongyan. This report was prepared by a study group of and published by the United States Air Force.

3. AYRES, R.U.: Environmental effects of nuclear weapons. Croton-on-Hudson, New York: Hudson Institute, Report No. HI-518-RR, 1965: 3 Vols. 392 pp.

This report considers the environmental impact of nuclear explosions on both the natural environment (Volume I) and agricultural ecosystems (Volume II). Volume III consists of a 25-page summary of Volumes I and II.

4. BACH, M.: Forêts mitraillées en Lorraine /Machine-gunned forests in Lorraine/. Revue Forestière Française 27, 1975: pp. 217-222.

A description of the damage to the forests of north-eastern France still in evidence today that resulted from the destructive military activities of World War II and even of World War I. The study area included ca. 170 thousand hectares of managed forest (three-quarters of it deciduous). Most of the long-term damage was the result of artillery shells or machine gun bullets. A map of the area is included and the damage is quantified.

5. BAKER, R.H.: Some effects of the war on the wildlife of Micronesia. Transactions of the North American Wildlife Conference 11, 1946: pp. 205-213.

It was found that the major adverse effects of World War II on the avian and mammalian wildlife of Micronesia was via a decimation of the vegetation and other components of the animals' habitat. Islands included in the study were Peleliu (in the Carolines), Kwajalein (in the Marshalls), Guam and Saipan (in the Marianas) and Iwo Jima (slightly north of Micronesia). It was observed that the Marianas mallard (Anas oustaleti) had been extirpated from Guam by military activities and that the entire species was thereby placed in jeopardy. The introduced sambar deer (Rusa unicolour) increased in numbers on Guam presumably owing to reduced hunting pressures resulting from the war. (See also the articles by Donaghho, 1950 and by Fisher & Baldwin, 1946.)

6. BARNABY, F.: Spread of the capability to do violence: an introduction to environmental warfare. Ambio 4, 1975: pp. 978-985.

Nuclear, chemical and biological weapons and their delivery systems are described and tabulated. Main emphasis is placed on their destructive abilities, increasing sophistication and continuing spread to additional nations. This is one of a group of articles edited by L. Kristoferson, 1975, q.v.

7. _____ : Environmental warfare. Bulletin of the Atomic Scientists 32 (5), 1976: pp. 36-43.

A review and assessment of environmental manipulations that have been employed for hostile military purposes or else have been suggested as future possibilities. Numerous potential techniques are presented in tabular form.

8. BARNABY, F.: Towards environmental warfare. New Scientist 69, 1976: pp. 6-8. Reprinted in: Current 1976 (182): pp. 55-59.

A brief survey of environmental manipulations for hostile purposes together with a summary of the environmental impact of United States operations during the Second Indochina War.

9. BAUER, E.; GILMORE, F.R.: Effect of atmospheric nuclear explosions on total ozone. Reviews of Geophysical and Space Physics 13, 1975: pp. 451-458.

An analytical review of ozone depletion in the stratosphere brought about by the oxides of nitrogen generated by thermonuclear explosions. The analysis is based upon data from the United States and Soviet test series during 1961-1962, the French testing in 1970, a review of the literature (33 citations) and theoretical calculations. It is concluded that the depletion appears to be real enough, but only of the order of several per cent.

10. BENSEN, D.W. & SPARROW, A.H. (eds.): Survival of food crops and livestock in the event of nuclear war. Washington: U.S. Atomic Energy Commission, 1971; 745 pp. Symposium Series No. 24.

A compilation of 43 separately authored articles dealing with the impact of nuclear war on agriculture, divided into the following five groups: properties of radio-active fall-out (8 articles); effects on livestock (12 articles); effects on plants (9 articles); effects on agricultural and natural ecological communities (9 articles); and considerations in agricultural defence planning (5 articles). An additional amount of relevant materials is presented in two appendices. Considerable attention is given in this monograph not only to the effects of gamma radiation but also to those of beta radiation.

11. BIDINIAN, L.J.: Combined allied offensive against the German civilian 1942-1945. Lawrence, Kansas: Coronado Press, 1976: 284 pp. + 44 pl.

An account of the United States and British area bombing operations against German cities during World War II which puts more emphasis on the impact on the civilian population as such than do the official U.S. Strategic Bombing Survey Reports (for which see MacIsaac, 1976).

12. BILES, R.E.: Bombing as a policy tool in Vietnam: effectiveness, Washington: U.S. Senate Committee on Foreign Relations, 1972: 29 pp. Pentagon Papers Staff Study No. 5.

This paper analyses the "effectiveness" of the United States strategic and interdiction bombing during 1965-1968 of North Viet Nam in the Second Indochina War, doing so on the basis of the extensive documentation in the so-called Pentagon Papers. It was concluded one reason for the limited effectiveness of the bombing was that, as an agricultural country, North Viet Nam provided an "extremely poor target" for air attack. Nevertheless, by 1968 about half a million civilians, including women and children, were working to repair damage done by air attacks. The value of foreign aid received during the first period of bombing exceeded the value of the facilities destroyed. Societal adjustments to the bombing were sufficiently effective to maintain living standards, meet transportation requirements and improve military capabilities.

13. BLACKETT, P.M.S.: Military and political consequences of atomic energy. London: Turnstile Press, 1948: 216 pp.

Data are presented from the World War II allied bombing of Germany which show that the decline in war production was not as great as had been expected by the British strategists. This book was published in the U.S.A. under the title of Fear, war and the bomb (New York: Whittlesey House, 249 pp., 1949). A Russian translation has also been published.

14. BOND, H. (ed.): Fire and the air war. Boston: National Fire Protection Association International, 1946: 260 pp.

A collection of 15 separately authored chapters on various aspects of incendiary (including nuclear) bombing during World War II, with very detailed accounts of the impact on urban areas in both Germany and Japan. This is one of the most comprehensive sources available on the subject.

15. BRANFMAN, F. (ed.): Voices from the Plain of Jars: life under an air war. New York: Harper & Row, 1972: 160 pp.

An extraordinarily moving series of first-person accounts in the form of brief essays and drawings by civilian primitive Laotian hill-tribesmen (montagnards) who had been subjected to repeated heavy bombing raids during the Second Indochina War.

16. CHANDLER, C.C.; STOREY, T.G. & TANGREN, C.D.: Prediction of fire spread following nuclear explosions. Washington: U.S. Forest Service, Research Paper No. PSW-5, 1963: 110 pp.

A study of nearly 2,000 wild fires in the United States (including an analysis of the extant weather conditions in relation to fire spread), supported by some 30 interviews with fire experts and the review of 149 publications. Guidelines are presented for predicting the behaviour of mass fires following nuclear attack. A summary of this study has been published separately by the senior author as U.S. Forest Service Research Note No. PSW-22, 8 pp., 1963.

17. CHOWDHURY, A.K.M.A. & CHEN, L.C.: Dynamics of contemporary famine. Dacca, Bangladesh: Ford Foundation Report No. 47, 1977: 32 pp.

A description, inter alia, of the causes and demographic impact of the famine that resulted from the Bangladesh War of Independence of 1971 (a war that resulted in between one to three million Bengali fatalities and in the displacement of perhaps ten million). Several mutually reinforcing interactions between infection and malnutrition and among births, deaths, and migrations were found to contribute to the impact of the acute nutritional crisis.

18. CLARK, R.S. (ed.): Effect of the war on the stocks of commercial food fishes. Copenhagen: Conseil Permanent International pour l'Exploration de la Mer, Rapports et Procès-Verbaux des Réunions No. 122, 1947: 62 pp.

A collection of eight separately authored investigations that describe the effects of World War II on about a dozen important fisheries on the Atlantic continental shelf of Europe. A comparison of the pre-war period (1937-1939) with the post-war period (1946) in most instances revealed an increased fish density (both in terms of numbers and individual sizes), presumably owing to reduced wartime fishing pressures. Substantial increases were reported especially for haddock (Melanogrammus aeglefinus), plaice (Pleuronectes platessa), ling (Molva molva) and hake (Merluccius merluccius).

19. CONARD, R.A. et al.: Twenty-year review of medical findings in a Marshallese population accidentally exposed to radio-active fallout. Upton, New York: Brookhaven National Laboratory, Publication No. BNL50424, 1975: 154 pp.

The early fall-out from the 15 MT thermonuclear test device detonated at Bikini (in the Marshalls, Micronesia) on 1 March 1954 exposed well over 100 persons to high levels of radio-activity (of the order of 200 R or more). Included among these were 89 Marshallese living on Rongelap atoll and 23 Japanese on a passing fishing vessel, the Lucky Dragon. Several deaths as well as a substantial number of tumours, some of them malignant, are attributable to this exposure. Included are an especially high frequency of thyroid tumours among those who were in utero or infants at the time. The bulk of this report reviews the continuing observations on the exposed Marshallese, based on both published (177 citations) and unpublished materials. Appendix 3 (pp. 89-93), by T. Kumatori, summarizes the studies on the exposed Japanese.

20. CRAFT, T.F.: Effects of nuclear explosions on watersheds. American Water Works Association Journal 56, 1964: pp. 846-852.

The effects of a low-altitude air burst by a nuclear weapon on a forested watershed (catchment area) are postulated. The major damage would be from the blast wave (resulting in tree blow-down) and from the thermal radiation (resulting in mass fires). Both runoff and erosion would be increased to undesirably high levels. The water would be radio-actively contaminated.

21. DONAGHHO, W.R.: Observations of some birds of Guadalcanal and Tulagi. Condor 52, 1950: pp. 127-132.

The major adverse impact of World War II on the birds of the Melanesian Solomon Islands of Guadalcanal and Tulagi was concluded to have been via vegetational and other habitat disturbance. Observations are presented on the successional recovery of war-torn jungle areas. (See also the articles by Baker, 1946 and by Fisher & Baldwin, 1946.)

22. EBERHARDT, L.L.: Some ecological aspects of nuclear war. Washington: U.S. Atomic Energy Commission, Report No. TID-23939, 1967: 29 pp.

A literature review (with 35 citations) of the ecological aspects of nuclear war. It is concluded that available information on the workings and interactions within ecosystems is insufficient to permit definitive conclusions. Concern is expressed over the possible consequences of nuclear war on weather and climate and over combined effects of radiation and disease.

23. EDVARSON, K.: Radioecological aspects of nuclear warfare. Ambio 4, 1975: pp. 209-210.

A brief discussion of the human casualties that would result from the nuclear radiation resulting from nuclear weapons, including considerations of both close-in and distant casualties. This is one of a group of articles, edited by L. Kristoferson, 1975, q.v.

24. ERVIN, F.R.; GLAZIER, J.B.; ARONOW, S.; NATHAN, D.; COLEMAN, R.; AVERY, N.; SHOHET, S. & LEEMAN, C.: Medical consequences of thermonuclear war. I. Human and ecologic effects in Massachusetts of an assumed thermonuclear attack on the United States. New England Journal of Medicine 266, 1962: pp. 1,127-1,137.

An examination of the postulated consequences of a 20 MT thermonuclear ground burst in the heart of Boston. The major focus of the article is on the medical and public health consequences of such an event, but ecological effects are also noted. (For a somewhat similar treatment of New York City, see the book by Stonier, 1964.)

25. FALK, R.A.: This endangered planet: prospects and proposals for human survival. New York: Random House, 1971: 497 pp.

The major theme of this perceptive, well-documented and thought-provoking treatise is that the global environment has deteriorated to such an extent that it has now become crucial that environmental considerations be given a dominant position in national and especially international affairs. The four dimensions of danger to the world ecology are concluded to be: the war system; the population explosion; an insufficiency of natural resources; and environmental (pollutional) overload. Subjects that receive major attention include the world order of today, the quest for world peace, attempts to bring about a new peaceful and environmentally sound world order and the prospects for attaining this elusive goal.

26. FEDOROV, E.K.: Disarmament in the field of geophysical weapons. Scientific World 19(3-4), 1975: pp. 49-54.

An analysis of the potential feasibility of various environmental manipulations suitable for hostile military purposes. It is concluded that a number of sorts of significant climatic manipulations are indeed within the realm of possibility for the foreseeable future. It is urged that an international agreement be reached to ban such military activities while these forms of warfare have not as yet been developed. (This journal is also published in French, German, Russian and Esperanto.)

27. FISHER, H.I. & BALDWIN, P.H.: War and the birds of Midway atoll. Condor 48, 1946: pp. 3-15.

A detailed survey of the battle impact of World War II on the Hawaiian Island of Midway (in Polynesia) and thus an informative summary of the military impact on the specialized biota of islands. The most serious impact on the fauna is via the upheaval of the habitat, the authors having observed an almost linear relationship. The war-caused extinction of the Laysan rail (Porzanula palmeri) is reported here as is the probable extinction of the Laysan finch (Telespiza cantans) and the local extirpation of the brown booby (Sula leucogaster plotus). (See also the articles by Baker, 1946 and by Donaghho, 1950.)

28. GANS, B.: Biafran relief mission. Lancet 1969(1), 1969: pp. 660-665.

Report of the medical consequences of the Nigerian Civil War of 1967-1970 by a member of the British paediatric relief team who spent ten weeks (November 1968-January 1969) in blockaded Biafra with its eight million inhabitants, half of whom were children. Some 21 months of siege resulted in the death by starvation of an estimated one-and-a-half million Ibos and other Biafrans. (See also the article by Mayer, 1969.)

29. GATES, P.W.: Agriculture and the Civil War. New York: A.A. Knopf, 1965: 383 + 13 pp. + 8 pl. + 1 map.

This monograph examines in some detail one of the major United States strategies during the U.S. Civil War of 1861-1865 to subdue the rebellious southern Confederacy, that of starving the entire population. A combination of blockade and scorched-earth tactics was employed, including the systematic destruction of railroads, of crops and food stores and of farm machinery.

30. GEORGIEVSKI, A.S. & GAVRILOV, O.K.: /Public health problems and consequences of wars./ (In Russian) Moscow: Medicina, 1975: 256 pp.

A detailed examination of the impact of war on public health, epidemics, nutrition and demography. Whereas much of the book is concerned with the impact of conventional wars over a fairly long historical period (with important statistical information particularly in regard to wars involving Imperial Russia and the Soviet Union), there are separate chapters examining the possible impact of nuclear, chemical and biological warfare on human populations and the biosphere. A valuable bibliography of relevant Soviet literature is included.

31. GLASSTONE, S. & DOLAN, P.J.: Effects of nuclear weapons. 3rd. ed. Washington: U.S. Departments of Defence & Energy, 1977: 653 pp. + slide rule.

This is the basic technical source for the description of nuclear weapons and their divers effects. Separate treatments are included for air bursts (both low and high altitude), surface bursts on land and sea, underground bursts and underwater bursts. Detailed attention is given to the several important forms of energy release - including the blast wave, the thermal pulse, nuclear radiation and radio waves - and their effects on Man and his artefacts. Little attention is given to environmental damage per se, but the wealth of information given is presented in such a way that it lends itself to apropos extrapolation. The prior (1964) edition continues to be useful for its treatment of radiological warfare, its compilation of nuclear explosions, and other omissions of the new edition.

32. GOLDBLAT, J.: Prohibition of environmental warfare. Ambio 4, 1975: pp. 186-190. Summarized in: SIPRI Yearbook 1976, pp. 83-84.

An analysis of the USSR/U.S.A. draft treaty of 21 August 1975 that would prevent those environmental manipulations for hostile purposes having widespread, long-lasting or severe effects. Serious shortcomings are pointed out. (A very similar treaty was opened for signature on 17 May 1977, analysed by J. Goldblat, 1977, q.v.) This is one of a group of articles edited by L. Kristoferson, 1975, q.v.

33. _____: Environmental warfare convention: How meaningful is it? Ambio 6, 1977: pp. 216-221.

An analysis of the "Convention on the Prohibition of Military or any other Hostile Use of Environmental Modification Techniques" opened for signature by the United Nations on 18 May 1977. This treaty would prohibit any hostile use of environmental modification techniques having widespread, long-lasting or severe effects. The author concludes that the treaty is inadequate for the prevention of environmental warfare since it proscribes mainly imaginary techniques and condones those which are feasible. (See also the earlier article by Goldblat, 1975.)

34. GRANVILLE, P.: Perspectives de la guerre météorologique et géophysique: un example concret: les opérations de pluies provoquées en Indochine /Perspectives on meteorological and geophysical warfare: a concrete example: the rain-provoking operations in Indochina/. Défense Nationale 31(1), 1975: pp. 125-140.

An evaluation of numerous possible hostile environmental manipulations including, inter alia, those involving fog, rain, tropical cyclones, the polar ice caps, stratospheric ozone, earthquakes, tsunamis and electromagnetic radiation. Two case histories are provided as well, namely the hostile rain-making and rural wildfire operations carried out by the United States during the Second Indochina War.

35. HAMPE, E. (ed.): Zivile Luftschutz im zweiten Weltkrieg: Dokumentation und Erfahrungsbericht über Aufbau und Einsatz /Civil air defence during World War II: documentation and first-person accounts on construction and defence7. Frankfurt-am-Main: Bernard & Graefe Verlag für Wehrwesen, 1963: 627 pp.

Very detailed and well-documented accounts of the impact of Allied bombing on German cities during World War II and the German civil defence efforts.

36. HAMPSON, J.: Photochemical war on the atmosphere. Nature 250, 1974: pp. 189-191.

It is suggested on the basis of calculations that high-altitude nuclear explosions would substantially deplete the ozone content of the stratosphere through the generation of oxides of nitrogen (being much more effective in this regard than low-altitude explosions). This ozone depletion would permit a larger fraction of the ultra-violet portion of the solar spectrum to reach the earth's surface with potentially disastrous effects on plants, animals and Man. (See also the article by Whitten & Borucki, 1975.)

37. HARRIS, M.: Ecology, demography and war. In: Harris, M., Culture, man and nature: an introduction to general anthropology. New York: T.Y. Crowell, 1971: 660 pp.: pp. 200-234 (Chapter 10).

A useful introduction to the relationships between the carrying capacity of the land, human population densities and war. Included are separate sections that deal with: warfare and population pressure among hunters and gatherers; warfare among agriculturalists; adaptive and maladaptive aspects of primitive warfare; and warfare in the modern world. In some primitive societies warfare has served to maintain a degree of balance between resources and population density, but in modern societies warfare cannot be regarded as an ecologically adaptive form of population control. The author concludes that, to the extent that the industrial nations benefit economically and politically from the continuing poverty and weakness of the underdeveloped world, alternatives to war and revolution may be inadequate for bringing about a more favourable balance between population and carrying capacity among the peoples of the underdeveloped nations.

38. HINES, N.O.: Proving ground: an account of the radiobiological studies in the Pacific, 1946-1961. Seattle: University of Washington Press, 1962: 366 pp.

The historical and biological aspects of the multi-faceted long-term studies of ecological damage and recovery that were carried out by the University of Washington Radiation Biology Laboratory at the U.S. nuclear test sites in the Marshall Islands (in Micronesia) at Bikini and Enewetak (Eniwetok) are described at length.

39. HOLMBERG, B.: Biological aspects of chemical and biological weapons. Ambio 4, 1975: pp. 211-215.

The toxicology of several chemical anti-personnel and anti-plant agents is surveyed, including delayed effects. The environmental impact of chemical anti-plant agents is reviewed on the basis of the Second Indochina War experience. This is one of a group of articles edited by L. Kristoferson, 1975, q.v.

40. HORTON, A.M.: Weather modification: a Pandora's box? Air Force Magazine 58(2), 1975: pp. 36-40.

A review of weather-modification capabilities (with emphasis on Soviet advances in the field) as these pertain to applications to hostile military purposes. It is concluded that there is no present danger of the cold war becoming wet or windy, but that there is a vast potential for environmental catastrophe.

41. HUISKEN, R.H.: Consumption of raw materials for military purposes. Ambio 4, 1975: pp. 229-233. Summarized in: SIPRI Yearbook 1976, pp. 95-101.

It is shown that today the world diverts annually to military use a quantity of resources representing about 6 per cent of total world output, equivalent to the combined gross national products of the 65 countries that comprise Latin America and Africa. The emphasis is on natural resource (raw material) consumption, which is considered a loss to the world community. This is one of a group of articles edited by L. Kristoferson, 1975, q.v.

42. IKLE, F.C.: Social impact of bomb destruction. Norman, Oklahoma: University of Oklahoma Press, 1958: 250 pp. + 10 ph.

A study of the sociological and demographical impacts of bomb destruction based upon the bombing of cities during World War II, primarily in Germany, Japan and Poland. The study is based upon data gathered by the author and on the U.S. Strategic Bombing Survey (cf. MacIssac, 1976). It is concluded that there is not a "one-to-one" relationship between the extent of physical destruction and social effects. For example, the policy of "dehousing" the civilian population by means of bombing did not produce a population exodus until some 25 per cent of the housing in German cities (or 10 per cent in Japanese cities) was destroyed. This was due to what the author describes as the "elasticity" of resources: resources - including accommodations - could be diverted from less important to more important tasks or uses. The war was seen to provoke a great deal of adaptive social behaviour, much of it carried out on a volunteer basis by individuals or organizations. The final chapter (Chapter 9, pp.203-232) deals with post-war problems of recovery and reconstruction. For a brief treatment of the subject, see the author's "Effect of war destruction upon the ecology of cities" in Social Forces 29, 1951: pp. 383-391.

43. Inter-allied Psychological Study Group: Psychological problems of displaced persons. London: UNRRA (United Nations Relief & Rehabilitation Administration), European Office, Welfare Division, 1945: 34 pp.

This mimeographed report - which argues that human beings are the single most important constituent of the environment - gives an excellent overview of the problems of persons whose lives were disrupted in Europe by World War II. It discusses the problems of displaced adults and children: the problems, for example, of mothers who have been forced to prostitute themselves in order to feed their children; of overcrowding and loss of privacy in camps and other makeshift accommodations; of other aspects of demoralization; and of various aspects of the task of rehabilitation. This report was prepared by an international group of eight psychiatrists, sociologists and social workers and was edited by J. Rickman. The findings deserve wide distribution.

44. IRVING, D.: Destruction of Dresden. London: William Kimber, 1963: 255 pp.

A detailed account of the background to and actual World War II allied air raid of February 1945 on Dresden. Prior to the war Dresden had been a cultural centre and one of the world's most beautiful cities. The raid destroyed much of the city. Moreover, with about 135,000 fatalities, this was perhaps the most destructive bombing raid in history in terms of human life.

45. JANIS, I.L.: Air war and emotional stress: psychological studies of bombing and civilian defense. New York: McGraw-Hill, 1951: 280 pp.

A discussion of the psychological impact of air attacks on human populations, drawn primarily from the experience of the British and German civil populations during World War II.

46. JASANI, B.M.: Environmental modifications: new weapons of war? Ambio 4, 1975: pp. 191-198. Summarized in: SIPRI Yearbook 1976: pp. 73-81, pp. 87-90. Summarized in: SIPRI. 1976. Armaments and disarmament in the nuclear age: a handbook. Stockholm: Almqvist & Wiksel, 308 pp.: pp. 134-138.

An exposition of the basic meteorological and other geophysical processes that must be understood and mastered before environmental manipulations for hostile purposes become feasible. Among the processes examined for possible manipulation are rain, fog, lightning, hurricanes, electro-magnetic radiation, earthquakes and tsunamis. The feasibility of most sorts of suggested means of environmental warfare is doubted. This is one of a group of articles edited by L. Kristoferson, 1975 q.v.

47. JOHNSTON, H.; WHITTEN, G. & BIRKS, J.: Effect of nuclear explosions on stratospheric nitric oxide and ozone. Journal of Geophysical Research 78, 1973: pp. 6,107-6,135.

A detailed technical analysis of the effect on stratospheric ozone level of oxides of nitrogen injected into the atmosphere by nuclear explosions. The level and extent of such injection resulting from the United States and Soviet test explosions during 1961-1962 were inferred from the recorded levels of ^{90}Sr. An examination of global ozone levels recorded for 1960-1970 suggests that the explosions had resulted in a temporary 5 per cent reduction in stratospheric ozone.

48. KENNEDY, E.M.: Aftermath of war: humanitarian problems of southeast Asia. Washington: U.S. Senate Committee on the Judiciary, 1976: 589 pp.

The most recent and one of the most extensive reports prepared for the U.S. Senate subcommittee on the human impact of the Second Indochina War. (Earlier reports go back over a ten-year period.) This is undoubtedly among the most detailed sources available on the social impact of that war. In particular it reproduces in full reports of the World Health Organization and United Nations missions to Indochina, reports that otherwise received only limited distribution. It also contains details of the aid programmes of international organizations as well as a selection of press reports on conditions in the countries of Indochina and Thailand following the conclusion of hostilities. This publication does not describe the ecological destruction resulting from the war in Indochina (for which see SIPRI, 1976), but it does describe the results of that destruction: the problems of moving back millions of peasant refugees from overcrowded cities with no economic basis to an extensively destroyed countryside; the problems of nutrition; an increase in diseases such as malaria; and so on. This publication goes a long way towards making up for the general dearth of information on the effects of war on developing countries. It makes it clear that one of the effects of war on a developing country may be to magnify the underlying problems of underdevelopment: rapid urbanization, disease, unemployment, inflation and a great many other social problems.

49. KRISTOFERSON, L. (ed.): War and environment: a special issue. Ambio 4(5-6), 1975: pp. 178-244. Swedish translation in Vår Lösen 67(4-5), 1976: pp. 153-264. Largely reprinted in: Strategic Digest 7(1-2), 1977: pp. 1-102.

This is a group of ten articles - and an appendix (pp. 234-244) that reprints legal and political documents - all pertaining to the interaction between war and the environment. The articles, each of which has a separate entry in the present bibliography, are by: F. Barnaby, K. Edvarson, J. Goldblat, B. Holmberg, R.H. Huisken, B.M. Jasani, M. Lumsden, I. Thorsson, A.H. Westing and H. York. This special double issue of Ambio was prepared in collaboration with SIPRI. Major portions of five of the articles (those by J. Goldblat, R.H. Huisken, B.M. Jasani, M. Lumsden and A.H. Westing) have appeared in SIPRI Yearbook 1976: pp. 72-101 (Chapter 4).

50. LAFARGE, H. (ed.): Lost treasures of Europe. New York: Pantheon, 1946: 39 pp. + 427 pl.

A catalogue of cathedrals, museums, monuments, statues, paintings and similar priceless art treasures that were destroyed by bombing and other military activities in Europe during World War II. The book, profusely illustrated by pre-war photographs, demonstrates very well the effect modern war can have on the cultural heritage of Man.

51. LEWALLEN, J.: Ecology of devastation: Indochina. Baltimore: Penguine, 1971: 179 pp.

A vivid, subjective first-person account of the human consequences of the heavy-handed U.S. tactics during the Second Indochina War against the land and people of rural South Viet Nam. The effects of bombing, of spraying chemical anti-plant agents and of landclearing with Rome-plough tractors are described as well as those of forced population relocation.

52. LITTAUER, R. & UPHOFF, N. (eds.): Air war in Indochina, rev. ed. Boston: Beacon Press, 1972: 289 pp.

An in-depth analysis of the massive and sophisticated employment of aircraft by the United States during the Second Indochina War. Separate chapters are devoted to the air wars waged against North Viet Nam, South Viet Nam, southern Laos, northern Laos and Cambodia. Other chapters examine the monetary costs, legal aspects and moral questions of this aspect of that war. A separate chapter (Chapter 8, pp. 91-96) and appendix (Appendix E, pp. 241-263) examine the ecological impact of the air war, including the effects of the air-delivered high-explosive munitions and of the chemical anti-plant agents (herbicides). This monograph constitutes an important study of the strategy of war in which a wealthy developed nation attempts to crush a poor underdeveloped adversary through lavish expenditures of remotely delivered munitions over wide areas.

53. LUMSDEN, M.: "Conventional" war and human ecology. Ambio 4, 1975: pp. 223-228. Summarized in: SIPRI Yearbook 1976: pp. 91-94.

This article points out that the origins of "ecological warfare" can be traced back to the efforts of colonial powers to "pacify" human populations in colonized territories. Drawing upon data from World War II and the Second Indochina War the author argues that, in spite of the enormous destructive capability of modern conventional weapon systems, human societies demonstrate a remarkable capacity to adapt to war. The data indicate, however, that a modern industrial society can rebuild its pre-war industrial capacity quicker than a poor agricultural society can regenerate its productive capacity. In the latter case the problem of wartime destruction is compounded by the underlying problem of underdevelopment. In so far as most recent wars have taken place in developing countries, this means that they are most detrimental to the very societies that can least afford them. This is one of a group of articles edited by L. Kristoferson, 1975, q.v.

54. LUND, D.H.: Revival of northern Norway. Geographical Journal 91, 1947: pp. 185-197 + 4 pl.

Norway was occupied by Germany during World War II. In late 1944, as an impediment to an expected Soviet advance, the Germans evacuated the resident local population of far northern Norway and destroyed the permanent structures remaining behind. This article describes the early post-war reconstruction efforts. It was written by the Director of the Office of Reconstruction of Finnmark County (the major zone of devastation). This case history demonstrates well the enormous effort required to restore a society that has been drastically disrupted by war.

55. MacDONALD, G.J.: Weather modification as a weapon. Technology Review 78(1-2), 1975-1976: pp. 56-63.

A review and analysis of rainfall manipulations for hostile purposes, including a review of the operations carried out by the United States during the Second Indochina War and an examination of the future potential and political implications of such activities.

56. MacISAAC, D. (ed.): United States Strategic Bombing Survey. New York: Garland Press, 1976: 10 Vols. (ca. 3,400 pp.).

Toward the close of World War II the United States instituted a massive study of the effects of the allied strategic bombing in Europe and the Pacific. The effects of high-explosive, incendiary and nuclear bombs were each examined in detail. Primary emphasis was placed upon the military, political, economic and social consequences of bombing cities and industrial centres, mostly in Germany and Japan. Some 850 military personnel and over 300 civilians under the leadership of F. D'Olier prepared six major reports, and more than 300 additional formal reports and several thousand background papers. Of the formal reports, published during 1945-1947, about 210 dealt with Europe and about 110 with Japan. Only about 80 of these were made generally available at the time and all have been out of print for several decades. In the present partial reprinting 20 reports deal with Europe (Volumes 1-6), including two of the three European summary reports; and 11 reports deal with the Pacific (Volumes 7-10), including the Pacific summary report. (Not included here, however, is the 317-page index volume to all of the several thousand reports that had been published by the USSBS in 1947.) A companion volume (Strategic Bombing in World War II: the story of the United States Strategic Bombing Survey) provides a history of this monumental and unique undertaking. (For the official British account of the strategic bombing of World War II, see Webster & Frankland, 1961.)

57. MARWICK, A.: War and Social Change in the Twentieth Century: A Comparative Study of Britain, France, Germany, Russia and the United States. New York: St. Martin's Press, 1974: 258 pp. + 5 pl.

An introduction to the modern historical study of the impact of war on society, based upon World Wars I and II. Four themes are focused upon: the destructive aspects of war; the extent to which war serves to test the effectiveness of a particular form of social organization; the impact of war on the degree of participation of the population in social processes; and the psychological aspects of the impact of war on soceity. Although the book is largely historical in concept, the author identifies himself in part with a more modern, sociological approach. An annotated bibliography of modern historical studies of war and society is included as well as a useful appendix on the use of archive film material.

58. MAYER, J.: Famine in Biafra. Post-Graduate Medicine 45(4), 1969: pp. 236-240.

Summary of the report of a mission to study nutritional problems in the Nigerian Civil War of 1967-1970. The situation is characterized as one of the great nutritional disasters of modern times. It is estimated that between one and two million Biafrans (primarily Ibos) died of starvation or malnutrition brought about by blockade and by the bombing of airfields and distribution centres through which relief supplies were brought in. The fatalities alone represent perhaps one-fifth of the Biafran population. The full study mission report is to be found in U.S. Congressional Record 115:4371-4382; 1969. (See also the article by Gans, 1969.)

59. NAGAI, T.: We of Nagasaki: the story of survivors in an atomic wasteland /Transl. from the Japanese by I. Shirato & H.B.L. Silverman/. New York: Duell, Sloan & Pearce, 1951: 189 pp.

A very moving, powerful first-person account of the tragic human sequelae to the nuclear bomb dropped by the United States during World War II on Nagasaki on 9 August 1945.

60. National Academy of Sciences: Effects of herbicides in South Vietnam. Washington: U.S. National Academy of Sciences, 1974: 20 Vols. (1,841 pp. + 8 maps).

The Second Indochina War will go down in military history as the one in which the United States introduced the massive and long-sustained employment of chemical anti-plant agents (herbicides) as a means of depriving a largely guerrilla enemy in South Viet Nam of forest concealment on the one hand and of food crops on the other. This report provides a lengthy though disjointed, uneven and poorly edited report of the forest destruction aspects of the programme. Part A (one volume of 398 pp.) presents the summary and conclusions of this several-year study and Part B (19 volumes) presents a series of working papers. Seven of the 19 working papers deal with lowland mangrove forest destruction and the remainder with upland (inland) forest destruction. It is concluded, inter alia, that it will take at least 100-120 years for the destroyed mangrove forests to recover. The report was prepared by A. Lang and 17 colleagues. The summary of the report has been reprinted in the U.S. Congressional Record 120: pp. 4,615-4,632; 1974.

61. _____: Long-term world-wide effects of multiple nuclear-weapons detonations. Washington: U.S. National Academy of Sciences, 1975: 213 pp.

A detailed evaluation based on an extensive literature survey of the long-term (20-year) effects of a war involving the detonation of nuclear weapons totalling 10,000 MT. Separate chapters deal with atmospheric effects, natural terrestrial ecosystems, managed terrestrial ecosystems, the aquatic environment, somatic effects on humans and genetic effects on humans. Most of the chapters give special emphasis to radio-active fall-out effects, photo-chemical effects, temperature effects and climatic effects. The report notes the possibility that ionizing radiation might cause widespread damage to crops and domestic animals, especially within the target countries. It was concluded that the most dangerous long-term world-wide effect of nuclear war would be the enhancement of ultra-violet radiation as a result of stratospheric ozone depletion (brought about by the generation of oxides of nitrogen). During the period it would take for the natural regeneration of the depleted ozone (of the order of 1-2 decades) widespread damage would be inflicted upon the earth's biota, including Man. It was further concluded that whereas Homo sapiens would survive a major nuclear exchange his civilization might not. This report was prepared by A.O.C. Nier and colleagues.

62. NEILANDS, J.B.; ORIANS, G.H.; PFEIFFER, E.W.; VENNEMA, A. & WESTING, A.H.: Harvest of death: chemical warfare in Vietnam and Cambodia. New York: Free Press, 1972: 304 pp.

Chapters 1 and 2 (by Neilands and Vennema, respectively) describe the use, toxicology and effects of the chemical anti-personnel agents employed by the United States in South Viet Nam during the Second Indochina War. Chapters 3 and 4 (by Pfeiffer and Orians and by Westing, respectively) describe the history, use and ecological effects of the chemical anti-plant agents, the former in South Viet Nam and the latter in Democratic Kampuchea. Numerous relevant documents are reprinted in an appendix. Chapter 4 (pp. 177-205) by Westing on "Herbicidal Damage to Cambodia" describes in some detail the extent of damage caused by herbicidal attack on rubber plantations, fruit trees, agricultural plants, livestock and humans. It thus provides one of the few descriptions of such attack on Man and nature in a rural, agricultural society.

63. NORDLIE, P.G. & GARRETT, R: Approach to the study of social and psychological effects of nuclear attack. McLean, Virginia: Human Sciences Research, Report No. HSR-RR-63/3-Rr, 1963: 452 pp.

The report contains a chapter on the physical effects of attacks using thermo-nuclear weapons and then attempts to draw up detailed guidelines for research on the possible societal, group and individual responses to such attack with a view to aiding civil defence planning. Thus the report is not merely descriptive of the effects of nuclear attack, and it is far from being a "handbook" for practising civil defence workers; rather it indicates the enormity of the research effort required to explore great areas of uncertainty with regard to the human effects of nuclear attack.

64. NORDLIE, P.G. & POPPER, R.D.: Social Phenomena in a Post-Nuclear Attack Situation: Synopses of Likely Social Effects of the Physical Damage. Arlington, Virginia: Human Sciences Research, 1961: 112 pp.

This booklet provides a useful overview of individual, social psychological and societal responses to disasters comparable with a nuclear attack. The aim of the study was to concentrate attention upon the interaction of physical and social effects and in particular upon the problem of "social damage assessment". Such assessment requires not only an inventory of damage, but also the tracing out of the ramifications of social disruption in order to attain the continued survival and recovery of society. This descriptive report was prepared for the U.S. Air Force.

65. O'CALLAGHAN, T.C.: Bibliography on geophysical, geochemical and geological effects of nuclear events. Alexandria, Virginia: General Publishing Services, Bibliographies in Science Series No. 1, 1973: 48 pp.

A bibliography with 519 citations arranged in alphabetical order, published primarily in the past decade or so. A limited subject index is appended.

66. OKADA, S. et al. (eds.): Review of thirty years study of Hiroshima and Nagasaki atomic bomb survivors. Journal of Radiation Research 16(suppl.), 1975: pp. 1-164.

A compilation of 17 separately authored review articles dealing with the long-term medical consequences of the World War II nuclear bombing by the United States of Hiroshima and Nagasaki in August 1945, grouped into the following three sections: dosimetry (6 articles); biological effects (9 articles); and future research and health surveillance (2 articles). This collection provides the most comprehensive overview of the subject currently available.

67. OLIVER, F.W.: Dust storms in Egypt and their relation to the war period, as noted in Maryut, 1939-1945. Geographical Journal 106, 1945-1946: pp. 26-49 + 4 pl.; 108: pp. 221-226 + 1 pl.

A detailed recording during 1939-1945 of the number and severity of dust storms occurring at a location about half way between El 'Alamein and Alexandria, Egypt, during World War II. Dust storms increased in number and severity as a result of military and related activities in the area including, inter alia, the Battle of El 'Alamein of October-November 1942. These activities had severely disrupted large surface areas and destroyed much of the vegetation, primarily the shrub Thymelaea hirsuta. The disturbed areas gave rise to dust storms with only half the wind velocity usually needed, thereby increasing their annual frequency by an order of magnitude. The problem persisted for the several years that it took for the re-establishment of a soil-stabilizing vegetative cover. It might be added that the presence of extensive mine fields contributed to the recovery of the vegetation by denying human access to large areas.

68. PAVLOV, D.V.: Leningrad 1941: the blockade /Transl. from the Russian 2nd ed. by J.C. Adams/. Chicago: University of Chicago Press, 1965: 186 pp. + 15 pl.

An authoritative description of the 900-day World War II siege of Leningrad by the Germans during 1941-1942. The author, who was in charge of both military and civilian food supplies in this besieged city of three million inhabitants, describes primarily the extraordinary problems of maintaining life under the conditions of the blockade. The author includes discussions of the administrative measures dealing with rationing, supplies, health and sanitation which - together with the co-operation of the population - limited deaths from starvation and disease to an estimated 632,000. This case study shows that ecological warfare can be carried out by means other than, for example, strategic bombing. Further, it illustrates the thesis that human beings and human societies are dependent upon an ecological relationship with their environment, but that when this environment is disrupted they are able to take partially compensatory adaptive measures.

69. PETTERSSON, L.: Det sårbara samhället /The vulnerable society/. Stockholm: Folk och Försvar, distributed by Rabén & Sjögren, 1977: 73 pp.

The secretary of a governmental group of experts reports on the increasing vulnerability of a highly industrialized society, Sweden, to crisis and war situations. The increasing vulnerability results from increasing dependence on imported raw materials and manufactured products, such as vital components for industry, as well as increasing socio-economic concentration. The report suggests measures to offset these trends, including decentralization, recycling of materials and so on - which correspond closely to conservation needs. For a brief treatment of the subject, see: L. Pettersson & S. Kronholm, 1975. Moderna samhällets sarbarhet /Modern society's vulnerability/. FOA Tidning 13(4): 3-7, 23 pp.

70. PFEIFFER, E.W.: Some effects of environmental warfare on agriculture in Indochina. Agriculture & Environment 3, 1976: pp. 271-281.

A summary, based upon on-site investigations, of the agricultural, horticultural and silvicultural damage caused by the United States during the Second Indochina War through the use of bombs, chemical anti-plant agents and land-clearing tractors (so-called Rome ploughs). The author concludes by supporting a resolution of the International Association for Ecology (INTECOL) that favours an international ban on environmental modifications for hostile military purposes.

71. POPPER, R.D. & LYBRAND, W.A.: Inventory of selected source materials relevant to integration of physical and social effects of air attack. Arlington, Virginia: Human Sciences Research, Report No. HSR-RR-60/4-SE, unpag.

This inventory of source materials - built around an annotated bibliography of 212 items - provides the background for a series of studies of the social dimensions of a possible nuclear attack. The present work is divided into three sections: various aspects of a projected thermo-nuclear attack, including the post-attack recovery period; societal, group or individual reactions to World War II bombings as well as to other large-scale disasters; and the development of analytical models and methods having potential utility in the further study of nuclear attack.

72. Red Cross, International Committee of the: Weapons that may cause unnecessary suffering or have indiscriminate effects. Geneva: International Committee of the Red Cross, 1973: 72 pp.

Various weapons having indiscriminate effects - including blast, fragmentation, time-delay and incendiary ones - are described with special emphasis on their medical effects. Brief descriptions of environmental impact are included. This report was prepared by the expert representatives of 19 nations.

73. Research Corporation of the University of Hawaii: Socio-economic study of Tinian, Mariana Islands District, Trust Territory of the Pacific Islands. Honolulu: University of Hawaii, Research Corporation, 1974: 417 pp.

This study constitutes a portion (Appendix III B) of a major "environmental impact statement" prepared for the U.S. Air Force regarding its plans to develop a large military base on the Micronesian island of Tinian. An historical introduction indicates some of the major ecological and social disturbances that have been inflicted upon the island and its population by a succession of occupying powers: the population was deported by the Spanish military authorities in the seventeenth century; it was enticed back by the Germans to work the copra plantations; the copra plantations were destroyed by the Japanese and replaced by sugar plantations; the island, like others in the Marianas, was severely damaged during World War II. At present it is inhabited by about 750 people. This study goes on to examine the economic and social impact on this small and young community if plans are realized to locate some 10,000 military and associated personnel on the island. Although peace-time as well as wartime military activities having had major environmental impacts have been the object of studies in the past, the present one is rare both in its depth and because it was made in advance of a potential military insult to the environment. As such it forms a commendable precedent for other national and international bodies. This study was prepared by M.W. Caulfield, L. Kelley and colleagues.

74. RUMPF, H.: Das war der Bombenkrieg: deutsche Städte im Feuersturm: ein Dokumentarbericht /That was the bombing war: German cities in a fire storm: a documentary account/. Oldenburg, Federal Republic of Germany: Gerhard Stalling, 1961: 208 pp. Translated as: Bombing of Germany. New York: Holt, Rinehart & Winston, 1963: 256 pp.

An account of the effects of allied bombing on Germany during World War II by one of the officials in charge of fire-fighting operations. Tables with damage estimates are included. The author has also published an earlier similar work: Hochrote Hahn /Crimson rooster/ (Darmstadt: E.S. Mittler, 167 pp. 1952).

75. RUSSELL, R.B. (ed.): Air, water, earth, fire: the impact of the military on world environmental order. San Francisco: Sierra Club, International Series No. 2, 1974: 71 pp.

A compilation of the following six separately authored chapters: I. The nature of military impacts on the environment (by R.B. Russell); II. Indochina: prototype of ecocide (by A.H. Westing); III. Nuclear explosives: potential for ecological catastrophe (by H. Scoville Jr.); IV. Environmental effects of chemical weapons (by S. Zolla & M. McClintock); V. Weather as a weapon (by E.B. Weiss); and VI. Humanitarianism and human survival (by R.B. Russell). The book also has a foreward by A. Myrdal.

76. SCHNEIDER, M.M.: Gegen den militärischen Missbrauch der Umwelt /Against the military misuse of the environment/. Deutsche Aussenpolitik 21, 1976: pp. 578-601.

A review of environmental manipulations for hostile military purposes together with an examination of the international negotiations aimed at proscribing them, the aims of which the author supports.

77. SCHULTZ, V.: References on Nevada test site ecological research. Great Basin Naturalist 26(3-4), 1966: pp. 79-86.

A bibliography with 161 citations dealing with the ecological research carried out at the atomic bomb test site in the Mohave (Great Basin) Desert of Nevada, U.S.A. (37°N 116°W). All of the references are to articles in the open literature, but some are of only limited circulation.

78. SHIELDS, L.M. & WELLS, P.V.: Effects of nuclear testing on desert vegetation. Science 135, 1962: pp. 38-40.

An examination of the extent of destruction and damage and of the rate of recovery following low-altitude aerial bursts of low-yield (mostly ca. 10 KT) in the Mohave (Great Basin) Desert at Yucca Flat, Nevada, U.S.A. (37°N 116°W). The extent of initial vegetational annihilation was of the order of 70-200 ha and that of damage, 400-1,400 ha. Reinvasion by pioneer species occurred within three to four years and full ecological recovery was expected to take many decades. This article should be read in conjunction with the one by Shields et al., 1963.

79. SHIELDS, L.M.; WELLS, P.V. & RICKARD, W.H.: Vegetational recovery on atomic target areas in Nevada. Ecology 44, 1963: pp. 697-705.

The annotation for this article is covered by the one for Shields & Wells, 1962, q.v. supra.

80. SIPRI (Stockholm International Peace Research Institute): Anti-Personnel Weapons. London: Taylor & Francis, 1978: (in press).

A basic reference source on anti-personnel weapons (small arms, grenades, conventional artillery and bombs, anti-personnel fragmentation bombs, mines and so on). It is written against the background of recent efforts at the inter-governmental level to restrict or prohibit the use of the more inhumane and indiscriminate of these weapons. Although the study is not primarily ecological in focus, the historical overview emphasizes the exponential increase in the fire-power available to front-line combat troops of the major powers and the trend towards increased area coverage. Ecological considerations are emphasized in the chapter on delayed-action munitions, including mines. It is pointed out that unexploded munitions result in a major, long-term environmental hazard and data are presented on the percentage of duds amongst various categories of munitions. The book contains a unique set of tables listing the quantities of cluster bombs and other anti-personnel munitions authorized for procurement for use in the Second Indochina War. This monograph was prepared by M. Lumsden.

81. _____: Dioxin: a potential chemical-warfare agent. SIPRI Yearbook 1977, 1977: pp. 86-102 (Chapter 4).

Dioxin or TCDD (2-, 3-, 7-, 8-tetrachlorodibenzo-p-dioxin), one of the most poisonous substances known to Man, is considered to be suited as a chemical-warfare agent for long-term area denial and other hostile purposes. The history and toxicology of this agent are reviewed. The behaviour of dioxin in the environment and its ecological consequences are examined on the basis of four episodes of contamination: in South Viet Nam during the Second Indochina War during 1961-1970; in north-western Florida, U.S.A., while testing chemical anti-plant warfare agents during 1962-1964; in eastern Missouri, U.S.A., during 1971; and in northern Italy during 1976. It is concluded that the adverse ecological consequences would be drastic in the light of the extreme toxicity, ecological mobility and great environmental persistence of dioxin. The social consequences would be drastic as well owing to the potential medical effects and to the long-lasting inability to utilize contaminated areas for agricultural or other civil pursuits. This chapter was prepared by A.H. Westing and K. Lohs.

82. _____: Ecological consequences of the Second Indochina War. Stockholm: Almqvist & Wiksell, 1976: 119 pp. + 8 pl.

Viet Nam, Democratic Kampuchea and Laos sustained enormous levels of environmental disruption during the Second Indochina War. The major instruments of destruction were bombs, chemical anti-plant agents and land-clearing tractors (Rome ploughs). Both the methods and extent of environmental damage from these sources are described and analysed in detail. There are also briefer treatments of the use for hostile purposes of rural fires and of cloud-seeding (rain-making) agents. A discussion of ecological recovery from war damage

is included. Very little attention is paid to the human consequences of the environmental damage described. This monograph was prepared by A.H. Westing. Excerpts appear in SIPRI Yearbook 1976: pp. 48-53; a summary appears in SIPRI Yearbook 1977: pp. 198-200. A Japanese translation is in the press (Tokyo: Iwanami Shoten Publishers).

83. _____: Environmental and ecological warfare. SIPRI Yearbook 1976, 1976: pp. 72-101 (Chapter 4).

Based on five articles that had originally appeared in a group of articles edited by L. Kristoferson, 1975, q.v. The articles, each of which has a separate entry in the present bibliography, were by: J. Goldblat, R.H. Huisken, B.M. Jasani, M. Lumsden and A.H. Westing.

84. _____: Incendiary weapons. Stockholm: Almqvist & Wiksell, 1975: 255 pp + 12 pl.

The basic source on incendiary weapons and their effects. Included are a history of the use of fire in warfare from antiquity to the present, with emphasis on the period during and since World War II, including especially the Korean War and the Second Indochina War. Modern incendiary weapons are described in detail as are thermal effects on human beings. Little attention is paid to the environment per se. This monograph was prepared by M. Lumsden.

85. _____: Military impact on the human environment. SIPRI Yearbook 1978, 1978: pp. 43-68 (Chapter 3).

This analysis begins with brief descriptions of the environmental impacts of several categories of warfare: conventional, nuclear, chemical, biological, and geophysical. The bulk of the chapter outlines the environmental impacts of warfare on the several major global habitats: temperate, tropical, desert, arctic, island and oceanic. It is concluded that the military abuses of the environment have the potential of reaching very substantial, not to say spectacular, proportions. Moreover, hostile environmental disruption is open to a priori criticism since its effect is unavoidably indiscriminate, uncontainable, and long-lasting. The first portion of the article is based upon the 1977 SIPRI monograph on Weapons of Mass Destruction and the Environment (q.v.); and the second upon the SIPRI monograph on Warfare in a Fragile World, to appear in late 1978 or early 1979. This chapter was prepared by A.H. Westing.

86. _____: Oil and security. Stockholm: Almquist & Wiksell, 1974: 197 pp.

A brief examination of the voracious military requirements for oil is included. This monograph was prepared by B. Heinebäck.

87. _____: Problem of chemical and biological warfare. Stockholm: Almqvist & Wiksell, 1971-1975: 6 Vols. 2,016 pp.

The definitive source for a wide range of technical information on chemical and biological weapons and warfare of the twentieth century. Little attention is paid to the environment per se. The titles of the separate volumes indicate the range of topics covered:

I. The rise of CB weapons, 1971, 395 pp.
II. CB weapons today, 1973, 420 pp.
III. CBW and the law of war, 1973, 194 pp.
IV. CB disarmament negotiations, 1920-1970, 1971, 412 pp.
V. The prevention of CBW, 1971, 287 pp.
VI. Technical aspects of early warning and verification, 1975, 308 pp.

These monographs were prepared by various researchers: I. by J.P. Robinson; II. by J.P. Robinson and colleagues; III. by A. Boserup; IV. by J. Goldblat; V. by A. Boserup and colleagues; and VI. by C-G Hedén.

88. SIPRI (Stockholm International Peace Research Institute): Prohibition of inhumane and indiscriminate weapons. SIPRI Yearbook 1973, 1973: pp. 132-163 (Chapter 5).

Efforts by the United Nations and the International Committee of the Red Cross to prohibit or restrict the use of certain inhumane or indiscriminate weapons are described. Particular attention is paid to incendiary weapons and data are presented on the use of incendiaries as strategic and tactical area weapons. Estimates are included of quantities used, areas destroyed and civilian casualties produced for World War II, the Korean War and the Second Indochina War. This chapter was prepared by M. Lumsden.

89. _____: Weapons of mass destruction and the environment. London: Taylor & Francis, 1977: 95 pp.

The extent and duration of environmental damage to be expected from nuclear, chemical, biological and selected environmental weapons are examined. Nuclear weapons are analysed in terms of their blast wave, thermal pulse and nuclear radiation and how these affect the geosphere, atmosphere and biosphere. The chemical and biological weapons examined include CS, VX, botulinal toxin, the anthrax bacillus and the yellow fever virus. Environmental weapons are illustrated by the use and effects of fire and of rain-making agents. This monograph was prepared by A.H. Westing.

90. SMELSER, N.J.: Theories of social change and the analysis of nuclear attack and recovery. McLean, Virginia: Human Sciences Research, Report No. HSR-RR-67/1-Me, 1967: 151 pp.

This monograph treats the problem of social recovery after nuclear attack as a special case of the general problem of social change. A number of general theories of short-term and long-term socially disintegrative processes are examined as well as theories of socially reconstructive and integrative processes. An attempt is made to integrate these theories within a framework that sees human societies as equilibrium systems which may be closed or opened with respect to outside influences. This integrated framework is then applied within the perspective of a nuclear attack. The theoretical analysis is of considerable interest in itself and has wider applications than that of a nuclear attack.

91. SOROKIN, P.A.: Man and Society in Calamity: The Effects of War, Revolution, Famine, Pestilence upon Human Mind, Behavior, Social Organization and Cultural Life. New York: E.P. Dutton, 1942: 352 pp.

This sociological study describes the typical effects of war, famine, pestilence and other calamities upon the human mind and socio-cultural life. It is concluded that these disasters contribute to an increase in the incidence of mental disturbances and emotional disorders which act as an additional burden on the afflicted society in the post-disaster period. This classic work has been republished by the Greenwood Press, New York, 1968.

92. SPOEHR, A.: Saipan: the ethnology of a war devastated island. Fieldiana: Anthropology 41, 1954: pp. 1-383.

A detailed account of the geography and history of Saipan and of the anthropology of the indigenous population. The devastation caused by World War II is described in brief (pp. 91-95) and this is followed by a more detailed account of the post-war recovery of the population and its economy (pp. 98-215).

93. STEIN, Z.; SUSSER, M.; SAENGER, G. & MAROLLA, F.: Famine and human development: the Dutch hunger winter of 1944-1945. New York: Oxford University Press, 1975: 284 pp.

A massively documented account of the long-term (permanent) physical and mental damage brought about by sustained substandard nutrition in human foetuses and infants. The study finds its basis in the effects of the food embargo that Germany imposed upon portions of the Netherlands in 1944-1945, during its occupation of that country during World War II. During the period of privation, population fertility declined and perinatal and infant mortality increased substantially. The major focus of the study is on adult males, surviving in 1971-1972, who had been in utero during 1944-1945, comparing such survivors from the famine city of Amsterdam with a control city in the south. For this group of survivors it was found that substandard prenatal nutrition had increased the frequency of central nervous system disorders although mental performance appeared to be essentially unaffected. For a preliminary report of this investigation, see Science 178: pp. 708-713; 180: pp. 133-136, 1972-1973.

94. STONIER, T.: Nuclear disaster. New York: Meridian, 1964: 225 pp.

An examination of the postulated consequences of a 20 MT thermonuclear bomb detonated over the heart of New York City. Both short-term and long-term consequences are explored. Two chapters deal with anticipated ecological upsets: Chapter 11 (pp. 121-135) focuses upon plants, insects and other animals whereas Chapter 12 (pp. 136-152) focuses upon climate and erosion. A preliminary version of this book appeared in the Annals of the New York Academy of Sciences 105: pp. 291-364; 1963. (For a somewhat similar treatment of Boston, see the article by Ervin et al., 1962.)

95. THORSSON, I.: Disarmament negotiations: What are they doing for the environment? Ambio 4, 1975: pp. 199-202.

A description by the chief Swedish delegate to the Geneva Conference of the Committee on Disarmament (CCD) of those negotiations that have pertained to the protection of the human environment. This is one of a group of articles edited by L. Kristoferson, 1975 q.v.

96. United Nations: Effects of the possible use of nuclear weapons and the security and economic implications for States of the acquisition and further development of these weapons. New York: United Nations, 1968: 76 pp.

An excellent brief treatment of the subject suggested by the title. Human ecology is well covered, although the impact on the environment per se is only indicated in passing. This monograph was prepared by M.A. Vellodi and colleagues.

97. _____ : Chemical and bacteriological (biological) weapons and the effects of their possible use. New York: United Nations, 1969: 100 pp.

An exceptionally useful summary of a variety of known and presumed chemical and biological agents. Included are descriptions of representative anti-personnel (both lethal and harassing), anti-animal and anti-plant agents, how they might be used in war and their effects on both the intended target and its environment. Medical, agricultural and ecological impacts are all covered in greater or lesser detail. This monograph was prepared by W. Epstein and colleagues. This book makes an excellent companion volume to the one by the World Health Organization, 1970 q.v.

98. _____ : Economic and social consequences of the arms race and of military expenditures; rev. ed. New York: United Nations, 1972: 90 pp.

A brief consideration is included of the effects of world-wide arms and other military expenditures on natural resources (raw materials). This monograph was prepared by G. Dolgu and colleagues.

99. _____ : Napalm and other incendiary weapons and all aspects of their possible use. New York: United Nations, 1973: 63 pp.

An excellent brief treatment of the use of fire in war. Emphasis is on the weapons and their medical effects. Succinct descriptions are included of the effects of incendiary attack on cities and of the use of such weapons on the battlefield and against environmental targets. This monograph was prepared by R. Björnerstedt and colleagues.

100. UNSCEAR (United Nations Scientific Committee on the Effects of Atomic Radiation): Ionizing radiation: levels and effects. New York: United Nations, 1972: 2 Vols., 447 pp.

This authoritative reference work provides detailed quantitative information on the sources of ionizing radiation (nuclear-weapon use, testing and accidents among them) and the effects of such radiation on Man (both somatic and genetic). Volume I is devoted to levels and Volume II to effects. Many tables and an extensive bibliography are included. A lengthy section (paragraphs 147-268) deals with atmospheric and surface nuclear explosions (including discussions of the transport of radio-active debris within the atmosphere, of internal radiation, of external radiation and of dose commitments). Another section (paragraphs 269-311) deals with underground and cratering nuclear explosions (including discussions of the sources of radio-activity, of contained experiments, of cratering experiments and of doses) This report was prepared by the scientific representatives of 15 nations.

101. URLANIS, B.: Wars and Population /Transl. from the Russian by L. Lempert/. Moscow: Progress Publishers, 1971: 320 pp.

This book contains extensive tabulations of the loss of human life (both military and civilian, both battle and non-battle) as a result of the direct and indirect effects of war and, as a consequence, of the influence of war on population dynamics. The data are drawn from a very wide variety of sources - for historical periods up to and including especially World Wars I and II - though mainly with reference to Europe during the last three-and-a-half centuries; there is brief reference to losses in some of the major post-World War II wars, but the available sources here are inadequate. In recent wars civilian losses have often exceeded losses of military personnel. In addition, excess mortality and a decline in birth rates may affect the age and sex composition of the population for decades. Although birth rates may be high in the post-war period, the proportion of the dependent fraction of the population (children, old people, invalids, etc.) increases relative to the productive fraction.

102. VAN DYKE, J.M.: North Vietnam's strategy for survival. Palo Alto, California: Pacific Books, 1972: 336 pp.

Taking as its point of departure the question as to why the massive United States bombing of North Viet Nam during the Second Indochina War failed to "bring that country to its knees", this book examines the impact of the bombing and the societal response to it. Extensive use is made of translated Vietnamese documents as well as of U.S. material. Although the human costs of the bombing were high, their impact was minimized through great efforts by the government and the population. A number of relatively straightforward measures were successfully instituted, such as evacuation of people and dispersal of industrial machinery, digging of simple shelters in large numbers, the decentralization of administration, the providing of grass-roots health services and the rationing of food and cloth.

103. VERWEY, W.D.: Riot control agents and herbicides in war: their humanitarian, toxicological, ecological, polemological, and legal aspects. Leyden: A.W. Sijthoff, 1977: 377 pp.

Part I of this work deals with chemical riot-control (harassing) agents, including their nature and toxicity; and Part II deals with chemical anti-plant agents (herbicides), including their nature, toxicity and environmental impact. Parts I and II draw heavily upon the Second Indochina War experience. Part III deals with the polemological (politico-military) aspects of the possession and use of these two classes of agents; and Part IV deals with the legal aspects. The major strength of the work lies in Part IV (Chapters 12-15, pp. 205-304).

104. VESTERMARK, S.D., Jr. (ed.): Vulnerabilities of social structure: studies of the social dimensions of nuclear attack. McLean, Virginia: Human Sciences Research, Report No. HSR-RR-66/21-Cr, 1966.

A compilation of five separately authored papers that is intended to provide planning and operating officials with information about possible patterns of social effects and societal vulnerabilities that would result from a nuclear attack on the United States. Among the subjects covered are demographic aspects, economic dimensions, political-administrative problems at the local governmental level and methodological issues with regard to the analysis of the social effects. There is a separate 40-page summary.

105. WEBSTER, C. & FRANKLAND, N.: Strategic air offensive against Germany 1939-1945. London: Her Majesty's Stationery Office, 1961: 4 Vols., 1,705 pp. + maps.

The official British account of the allied strategic bombing offensive against Germany during World War II. Volume I is entitled "Preparation", Volume II "Endeavour", Volume III "Victory", and Volume IV "Annexes and Appendices". Among those items of environmental concern are the appendices that summarize the findings of the British and U.S. Strategic Bombing Surveys, calculations of the tonnage of bombs required to inflict "decisive damage" on a populated city (for example, 3 tonnes per square kilometre or 1 tonne per 800 people at 50 per cent efficiency) and references to abortive plans and attempts to burn agricultural fields and forests. (For the official U.S. account of the strategic bombing of World War II, see MacIsaac, 1976.)

106. WEISBERG, B. (ed.): Ecocide in Indochina: the ecology of war. San Francisco: Canfield, Press, 1970: 241 pp. + 7 pl.

A collection of two dozen separately authored articles, most of them previously published, all dealing with social and ecological aspects of the Second Indochina War. They are divided into the following five groups: Introduction (1 article); Overview (4 articles); Earth below: destruction of the living landscape (6 articles); Destruction of a culture (9 articles); and From the other side (4 articles).

107. WEISS, E.B.: Weather control: an instrument for war? Survival 17, 1975: pp. 64-68.

A brief review of weather- (rain, fog) manipulation capabilities, their application to hostile military purposes and the legal and diplomatic implications of such actions.

108. WESTING, A.H.: U.S. food destruction program in South Vietnam. In: Browning, F. & Forman, D. (eds.). Wasted nations. New York: Harper & Row, 1972: 346 pp. pp. 21-25.

One of the continuing strategies of the United States during the Second Indochina War was to deny food to its largely guerrilla enemy in South Viet Nam. One of the important means by which it was attempted to accomplish this was through the aerial application of chemical anti-plant agents, often the herbicide dimethyl arsinic acid (code name, Agent Blue). The present article approximates the amount of food destroyed by this means alone during 1961-1971, largely in the Central Highlands of South Viet Nam: a very conservative calculation suggests that sufficient upland rice and other field crops were thus destroyed to provide the total diet for almost 900,000 people for a period of one year. Virtually all of the destroyed crops had been destined for civilian consumption. A briefer preliminary version of this article appeared in the New York Times, 12 July 1971, p. 27.

109. _____: Herbicides as weapons: a bibliography. Los Angeles: California State University Center for the Study of Armament and Disarmament, Political Issues Series 3(1), 1974: 36 pp.

A bibliography with 294 citations that covers the world literature on the military use for hostile purposes of chemical anti-plant agents (herbicides). By far the greatest number deal with the Second Indochina War. Included in the compilation are 45 items of limited circulation by the U.S. Department of Defense.

110. _____: Proscription of ecocide: arms control and the environment. Bulletin of the Atomic Scientists 30(1), 1974: pp. 24-27. Largely reprinted in SIPRI, 1976. Armaments and disarmament in the nuclear age: a handbook. Stockholm: Almqvist & Wiksell, 308 pp.: pp. 142-145.

An analysis is made of the traditional approaches to arms control and disarmament with reference to prohibiting environmental damage of the sort that occurred during the Second Indochina War. It is concluded that the traditional approaches - those focusing on Man per se, on geographical regions, or on the weapons themselves - have only limited applicability. It is suggested that a new approach is required to prevent serious ecological debilitation (so-called ecocide) by military means, one that focuses on the target rather than the technique, on the effect rather than the means.

111. _____: Environmental consequences of the Second Indochina War: a case study. Ambio 4, 1975: pp. 216-222. Summarized in: SIPRI Yearbook 1976: 82-83.

It is shown that limited warfare can result in widespread, long-lasting and severe environmental damage. This has been demonstrated by a study of the effects of high-explosive munitions (bombs and shells), chemical anti-plant agents (herbicides) and heavy land-clearing tractors (so-called Rome ploughs) as employed by the United States in South Viet Nam during the Second Indochina War, largely for the purpose of extended large-scale area denial. The ecological lesson to be learned is that the vegetation can be severely damaged or even destroyed with relative ease over extensive areas; that natural, agricultural and industrial-crop plant communities are all similarly vulnerable; and that the ecological impact of such actions is likely to be of long duration. Although the ecological damage to South Viet Nam was severe, the area-denial techniques used were of doubtful military success. It is therefore concluded that should a similar strategy be pursued in some future war, then the ecological damage can be expected to be far worse owing to the military necessity for a greatly expanded application of such techniques. This is one of a group of articles edited by L. Kristoferson, 1975, q.v.

112. WESTING, A.H.: Military impact on ocean ecology. Ocean Yearbook 1977, 1977: (in press).

This article examines the impact on the world ocean of military activities, both hostile and non-hostile, in relation to those of civil origin. Among the military abuses singled out for quantitative examination are underwater explosions, both conventional and nuclear, and contamination of the ocean with radio-active isotopes, chemical-warfare agents and oil. It is concluded that anthropogenic abuses of the world ocean are approaching a danger level and it is suggested that the military contribution to these abuses is one of the prime candidates for curtailment.

113. WHITTEN, R.C. & BORUCKI, W.J.: Possible ozone depletions following nuclear explosions. Nature 257, 1975: pp. 38-39.

A corroboration of the concerns expressed by Hampson, 1974, q.v., and an extension of his calculations to include low-altitude nuclear explosions.

114. WOODWELL, G.M. (ed.): Ecological effects of nuclear war. Upton, New York: Brookhaven National Laboratory, Publication No. 917, 1963: 72 pp.

A group of five articles: "Physical damage from nuclear explosions" (by C.F. Miller); "Effects of fire on major ecosystems" (by A. Broido); "Effects of ionizing radiation on ecological systems" (by G.M. Woodwell and A.H. Sparrow); "Ionizing radiation and homeostasis of ecosystems" (by R.B. Platt); and "Biological interactions associated with spruce budworm infestations" (by D.R. MacDonald). There is also a "Summary" (by E.P. Odum). This collection of papers is useful not only in clarifying the complex ecological problems involved in a nuclear holocaust, but also in defining the normal patterns of structure, function and development characteristic of natural ecosystems. Fire and nuclear radiation - two of the major effects of nuclear weapons - are especially well covered.

115. World Health Organization: Health aspects of chemical and biological weapons. Geneva: World Health Organization, 1970: 132 pp.

The consequences of employing the various major chemical and biological warfare agents are analysed with special reference to the public health, medical and psychosocial consequences. Included are descriptions of lethal, incapacitating, harassing, anti-plant and other chemical agents as well as viral, rickettsial, bacterial and fungal biological agents. The danger of epidemics, casualty estimates and the contamination of water supplies are among the topics singled out. This monograph was prepared by M. Kaplan and colleagues. This book makes an excellent companion volume to the one by the United Nations, 1969, q.v.

116. WRIGHT, Q.: Study of war: with a commentary on war since 1942. 2nd ed. Chicago: University of Chicago Press, 1965: 1,637 pp.

An exhaustive treatise on the theory, history, causes and prevention of war; the classic study in its field. Although the effects of war (aside from casualties) are essentially not covered, the book is nevertheless useful in the present context because of its extensive statistical information, much of it in tabular form.

117. YORK, H.: Nuclear "balance of terror" in Europe. Ambio 4, 1975: pp. 203-208.

A scenario of a nuclear war in western Europe between the NATO and Warsaw Pact nations. In short, Europe could be totally destroyed by such a war. Less than 600 Soviet missiles could eliminate virtually the entire urban population (by blast) and most of the suburban and rural population (by nuclear fall-out) of western Europe, plus a million more elsewhere in the world. This is one of a group of articles edited by L. Kristoferson, 1975 q.v.

UNESCO PUBLICATIONS: NATIONAL DISTRIBUTORS

Argentina — EDILYR S.R.L., Tucumán 1699 (P.B. 'A'), 1050, BUENOS AIRES.

Australia — *Publications:* Educational Supplies Pty. Ltd., Post Office Box 33, BROOKVALE 2100, N.S.W. *Periodicals:* Dominie Pty. Subscriptions Dept., P.O. Box 33, BROOKVALE 2100, N.S.W. *Sub-agent:* United Nations Association of Australia (Victorian Division), 2nd floor, Campbell House, 100 Flinders St., MELBOURNE 3000.

Austria — Dr. Franz Hain, Verlags- und Kommissionsbuchhandlung, Industriehof Stadlau, Dr. Otto-Neurath-Gasse 5, 1220 WIEN.

Belgium — Jean De Lannoy, 202, Avenue du Roi, 1060 BRUXELLES. CCP 000–0070823-13.

Benin — Librairie nationale, B.P. 294, PORTO NOVO.

Bolivia — Los Amigos del Libro: casilla postal 4415, LA PAZ; Perú 3712 (Esq. España), casilla postal 450, COCHABAMBA.

Brazil — Fundação Getúlio Vargas, Editora-Divisão de Vendas, caixa postal 9.052-ZC-02, Praia de Botafogo 188, RIO DE JANEIRO, R.J.

Bulgaria — Hemus, Kantora Literatura, boulevard Rousky 6, SOFIJA.

Burma — Trade Corporation no. (9), 550–552 Merchant Street, RANGOON.

Canada — Renouf Publishing Company Ltd., 2182 St. Catherine Street West, MONTREAL, Que., H3H 1M7.

Chile — Bibliocentro Ltda., Constitución n.° 7, Casilla 13731, SANTIAGO (21).

Colombia — Editorial Losada, calle 18A, n.° 7–37, apartado aéreo 5829, BOGOTÁ; Edificio La Ceiba, oficina 804, calle 52 n.° 47–28, MEDELLÍN.

Congo — Librairie Populaire, B.P. 577, BRAZZAVILLE.

Costa Rica — Librería Trejos S.A., apartado 1313, SAN JOSÉ.

Cuba — Instituto Cubano del Libro, Centro de Importación, Obispo 461, LA HABANA.

Cyprus — 'MAM', Archbishop Makarios 3rd Avenue, P.O. Box 1722, NICOSIA.

Czechoslovakia — SNTL, Spalena 51, PRAHA 1 (*Permanent display*); Zahranicni literatura, 11 Soukenicka, PRAHA 1. *For Slovakia only*: Alfa Verlag Publishers, Hurhanova nam. 6, 893 31 BRATISLAVA.

Denmark — Ejnar Munksgaard Ltd., 6 Nørregade, 1165 KØBENHAVN K.

Egypt — National Centre for Unesco Publications, 1 Talaat Harb Street, Tahrir Square, CAIRO.

El Salvador — Librería Cultural Salvadoreña, S.A., calle Delgado, n.° 117, apartado postal 2296, SAN SALVADOR.

Ethiopia — Ethiopian National Agency for Unesco, P.O. Box 2996, ADDIS ABABA.

Finland — Akateeminen Kirjakauppa, Keskuskatu 1, SF-00100 HELSINKI 10.

France — Librairie de l'Unesco, 7, place de Fontenoy, 75700 PARIS. CCP Paris 12598-48.

French West Indies — Librairie 'Au Boul' Mich', 1 Rue Perrinon *and* 66 Avenue du Parquet, 97200 FORT-DE-FRANCE (Martinique).

German Dem. Rep. — Buchhaus Leipzig, Postfach 140, 701 LEIPZIG or international bookshops in the German Democratic Republic.

Germany, Fed. Rep. of — S. Karger GmbH, Karger Buchhandlung, Angerhofstrasse 9, Postfach 2, D-8034 GERMERING/MÜNCHEN. *For scientific maps only*: Geo Center, Postfach 800830, 7000 STUTTGART 80. *For 'The Courier'* (German edition only): Colmantstrasse 22, 5300 BONN.

Ghana — Presbyterian Bookshop Depot Ltd., P.O. Box 195, ACCRA; Ghana Book Suppliers Ltd., P.O. Box 7869, ACCRA; The University Bookshop of Ghana, ACCRA; The University Bookshop of Cape Coast; The University Bookshop of Legon, P.O. Box 1, LEGON.

Greece — International bookshop (Eleftheroudakis, Kauffman, etc.).

Hong Kong — Swindon Book Co., 13–15 Lock Road, KOWLOON; Federal Publications (HK) Ltd., 5a Evergreen Industrial Mansion, 12 Yip Fat Street, Wong Chuk Hang Road, ABERDEEN.

Hungary — Akadémiai Könyvesbolt, Váci u. 22, BUDAPEST VI.

Iceland — Snaebjörn Jonsson & Co., H.F., Hafnarstraeti 9, REYKJAVIK.

India — Orient Longman Ltd., Kamani Marg, Ballard Estate, BOMBAY 400038; 17 Chittaranjan Avenue, CALCUTTA 13; 36a Anna Salai, Mount Road, MADRAS 2; B-3/7 Asaf Ali Road, NEW DELHI 1; 80/1 Mahatma Gandhi Road, BANGALORE 560001; 3–5–820 Hyderguda, HYDERABAD 500001. *Sub-depots*: Oxford Book and Stationery Co., 17 Park Street, CALCUTTA 700016; Scindia House, NEW DELHI 110001; Publications Section, Ministry of Education and Social Welfare, 511 C-Wing, Shastri Bhavan, NEW DELHI 110001.

Indonesia — Bhratara Publishers and Booksellers, 29 Jl. Oto Iskandardinata 111, JAKARTA; Gramedia Bookshop, Jl. Gadjah Mada 109, JAKARTA; Indira P.T., Jl. Dr. Sam Ratulangi 37, JAKARTA PUSAT.

Iran — Iranian National Commission for Unesco, Avenue Iranchahr Chomali no. 300, B.P. 1533, TEHRAN; Kra-razmie Publishing and Distribution Co., 28 Vessal Shirazi Street, Shahreza Avenue, P.O. Box 314/1486, TEHRAN.

Iraq — McKenzie's Bookshop, Al-Rashid Street, BAGHDAD.

Ireland — The Educational Company of Ireland Ltd., Ballymount Road, Walkinstown, DUBLIN 12.

Israel — Emanuel Brown, formerly Blumstein's Bookstores, 35 Allenby Road *and* 48 Nachlat Benjamin Street, TEL AVIV; 9 Shlomzion Hamalka Street, JERUSALEM.

Italy — Licosa (Librería Commissionaria Sansoni S.p.A.), via Lamarmora 45, casella postale 552, 50121 FIRENZE.

Jamaica — Sangster's Book Stores Ltd., P.O. Box 366, 101 Water Lane, KINGSTON.

Japan — Eastern Book Service Inc., C.P.O. Box 1728, TOKYO 10092.

Kenya — East African Publishing House, P.O. Box 30571, NAIROBI.

Republic of Korea — Korean National Commission for Unesco, P.O. Box Central 64, SEOUL.

Kuwait — The Kuwait Bookshop Co. Ltd., P.O. Box 2942, KUWAIT.

Lesotho — Mazenod Book Centre, P.O. MAZENOD.

Liberia — Cole & Yancy Bookshops Ltd., P.O. Box 286, MONROVIA.

Libyan Arab Jamahiriya — Agency for Development of Publication and Distribution, P.O. Box 34–35, TRIPOLI.

Luxembourg — Librairie Paul Bruck, 22 Grande-Rue, LUXEMBOURG.

Madagascar — Commission nationale de la République démocratique de Madagascar pour l'Unesco, Boîte postale 331, TANANARIVE.

Malaysia — Federal Publications Sdn. Bhd., Lot 8238 Jalan 222, Petaling Jaya, SELANGOR.

Malta — Sapienzas, 26 Republic Street, VALLETTA.

Mauritius — Nalanda Co. Ltd., 30 Bourbon Street, PORT-LOUIS.

Mexico — SABSA, Insurgentes Sur, n.° 1032-401, MÉXICO 12, D.F.

Monaco — British Library, 30, boulevard des Moulins, MONTE-CARLO.

Mozambique — Instituto Nacional do Livro e do Disco (INLD), Avenida 24 de Julho, 1921-r/c e 1° andar, MAPUTO.

Netherlands — N.V. Martinus Nijhoff, Lange Voorhout 9, 's-GRAVENHAGE; Systemen Keesing, Ruysdaelstraat 71–75, AMSTERDAM 1007.

Netherlands Antilles — Van Dorp-Eddine N.V., P.O. Box 200, Willenstad, CURAÇAO, N.A.

New Caledonia — Reprex S.A.R.L., Boîte postale 1572, NOUMÉA.

New Zealand — Government Printing Office, Government bookshops: Mulgrave Street, Private Bag, WELLINGTON; Rutland Street, P.O. Box 5344, AUCKLAND; 130 Oxford Terrace, P.O. Box 1721, CHRISTCHURCH; Alma Street, P.O. Box 857, HAMILTON; Princes Street, P.O. Box 1104, DUNEDIN.

Niger — Librairie Mauclert, B.P. 868, NIAMEY.

Nigeria — The University Bookshop of Ife; The University Bookshop of Ibadan, P.O. Box 286; The University Bookshop of Nsukka; The University Bookshop of Lagos; The Ahmadu Bello University Bookshop of Zaria.

Norway — *Publications*: Johan Grundt Tanum, Karl Johans gate 41/43, OSLO 1. *For 'The Courier'*: A/S Narvesens Litte-raturtjeneste, Box 6125, OSLO 6.

Pakistan — Mirza Book Agency, 65 Shahrah Quaid-e-azam, P.O. Box 729, LAHORE 3.

Peru — Editorial Losada Peruana, Jirón Contumaza 1050, apartado 472, LIMA.

Philippines — The Modern Book Co., 926 Rizal Avenue, P.O. Box 632, MANILA D-404.

Poland — ORPAN-Import, Palac Kultury, 00–901 WARSZAWA; Ars Polona-Ruch, Krakowskie Przedmiescie N° 7, 00–068 WARSZAWA.

Portugal — Dias & Andrade Ltda., Livraria Portugal, rua do Carmo 70, LISBOA.

Southern Rhodesia — Textbook Sales (PVT) Ltd., 67 Union Avenue, SALISBURY.

Romania — ILEXIM, Romlibri Str. Biserica Amzei no. 5-7, P.O.B. 134-135, BUCUREŞTI. *Periodicals (subscriptions)*: Rom-presfilatelia, Calea Victoriei nr. 29, BUCUREŞTI.

Senegal	La Maison du Livre, 13, avenue Roume, B.P. 20-60, DAKAR; Librairie Clairafrique, B.P. 2005, DAKAR; Librairie 'Le Sénégal', B.P. 1594, DAKAR.
Singapore	Federal Publications (S) Pte. Ltd., no. 1 New Industrial Road, off Upper Paya Lebar Road, SINGAPORE 19.
Somalia	Modern Book Shop and General, P.O. Box 951, MOGADISCIO.
South Africa	Van Schaik's Bookstore (Pty.) Ltd., Libri Building, Church Street, P.O. Box 724, PRETORIA.
Spain	MUNDI-PRENSA LIBROS S.A., Castelló 37, MADRID 1; Ediciones LIBER, Apartado 17, Magdalena 8, ONDÁRROA (Vizcaya); DONAIRE, Ronda de Outeiro, 20, Apartado de Correos, 341, LA CORUÑA; Librería AL-ANDALUS, Roldana, 1 y 3, SEVILLA 4; LITEXSA, Librería Técnica Extranjera, Tuset, 8–10 (Edificio Monitor), BARCELONA.
Sri Lanka	Lake House Bookshop, Sir Chittampalam Gardiner Mawata, P.O. Box 244, COLOMBO 2.
Sudan	Al Bashir Bookshop, P.O. Box 1118, KHARTOUM.
Sweden	*Publications*: A/B C.E. Fritzes Kungl. Hovbokhandel, Fredsgatan 2, Box 16356, 103 27 STOCKHOLM 16. *For 'The Courier'*: Svenska FN-Förbundet, Skolgränd 2, Box 150 50, S-104 65 STOCKHOLM.
Switzerland	Europa Verlag, Rämistrasse 5, 8024 ZÜRICH; Librairie Payot, 6, rue Grenus, 1211 GENEVA 11.
Thailand	Suksapan Panit, Mansion 9, Rajdamnern Avenue, BANGKOK; Nibondh and Co. Ltd., 40–42 Charoen Krung Road, Siyaeg Phaya Sri, P.O. Box 402, BANGKOK; Suksit Siam Company, 1715 Rama IV Road, BANGKOK.
Togo	Librairie Évangélique, P.B. 378, LOMÉ; Librairie du Bon Pasteur, B.P. 1164, LOMÉ; Librairie Moderne, B.P. 777, LOMÉ.
Turkey	Librairie Hachette, 469 Istiklal Caddesi, Beyoglu, ISTANBUL.
Uganda	Uganda Bookshop, P.O. Box 145, KAMPALA.
U.S.S.R.	Mezhdunarodnaja Kniga, MOSKVA, G-200.
United Kingdom	H.M. Stationery Office, P.O. Box 569, LONDON SE1 9NH; Government Bookshops: London, Belfast, Birmingham, Bristol, Cardiff, Edinburgh, Manchester.
United Rep. of Cameroon	Le secrétaire général de la Commission nationale de la République Unie du Cameroun pour l'Unesco, B.P. 1600, YAOUNDÉ.
United Rep. of Tanzania	Dar es Salaam Bookshop, P.O. Box 9030, DAR ES SALAAM.
United States	Unipub, Box 433, Murray Hill Station, NEW YORK, New York 10016.
Upper Volta	Librairie Attie, B.P. 64, OUAGADOUGOU; Librairie catholique 'Jeunesse d'Afrique', OUAGADOUGOU.
Uruguay	Editorial Losada Uruguay, S.A., Maldonado 1092, MONTEVIDEO.
Venezuela	Librería del Este, Av. Francisco de Miranda, 52, Edificio Galipán, Apartado 60337, CARACAS; La Muralla Distribuciones, S.A., 4a, Avenida entre 3a. y 4a. transversal, 'Quinta Irenalis' Los Palos Grandes, CARACAS 106.
Yugoslavia	Jugoslovenska Knjiga, Trg Republike 5/8, P.O. Box 36, 11–001 BEOGRAD; Drzavna Zalozba Slovenije, Titova C. 25, P.O.B. 50-1, 61–000 LJUBLJANA.
Zaire	La Librairie, Institut national d'études politiques, B.P. 2307, KINSHASA; Commission nationale zaïroise pour l'Unesco, Commissariat d'État chargé de l'Éducation nationale, B.P. 32, KINSHASA.